FLASH

For 'TITTERS' ENJOY THE READ
COBBER, DON'T FORGET WHEN THE
HORSE IS DEAD DISMOUNT.
I WISH YOU BOTH A LONG & HAPPY
LIFE TOGETHER.
        REGARDS.
            Dogs.
            RHLee

FLASHBACK

Echoes from a Hard War

PETER HARAN
ROBERT KEARNEY

NEW HOLLAND

First published in Australia in 2003 by
New Holland Publishers (Australia) Pty Ltd
Sydney • Auckland • London • Cape Town

14 Aquatic Drive Frenchs Forest NSW 2086 Australia
218 Lake Road Northcote Auckland New Zealand
86 Edgware Road London W2 2EA United Kingdom
80 McKenzie Street Cape Town 8001 South Africa

2 4 6 8 10 9 7 5 3 1

National Library of Australia Cataloguing-in-Publication Data:

Haran, Peter, 1948–.
Flashback: echoes from a hard war.

ISBN 1 74110 000 3.

1. Vietnamese Conflict, 1961-1975—Veterans—Australia.
2. Vietnamese Conflict, 1961-1975—Psychological aspects. I. Title.

959.70438

Publishing Manager: Anouska Good
Senior Editor: Monica Ban
Copy Editor: Sean Doyle
Designer: Karlman Roper
Reproduction: PICA
Printer: Griffin Press

This book was typeset in Bembo, Optima and Courier 10 pt

*Cover: Private Colin Cogswell photographed at Nui Dat before going on operations.
Cogswell was awarded the Military Medal for bravery in 1966.
Picture courtesy of Colin Cogswell*

FOREWORD

The experiences of soldiers in combat are unlike any others. This book shares some of those experiences drawn from the memories of Australian veterans of the Vietnam War.

Flashback presents a compelling collection of reminiscences, captured some thirty years after the events unfolded. They are stories that were etched into the memories of those who were there and have withstood the tests of time; resisting the modulating effects of bravado and 'war stories', or reflective silence and denial. They present enduring images, observations and memories with a striking clarity and intensity that resonates down to the present day.

Although these flashbacks are drawn from many soldiers, collectively they represent the story of any soldier who has seen combat. They provide a window through which the reader can look into a world that few Australians understand. It is a world full of paradoxes and mixed emotions; courage and fear, humour and sadness, pride and humility, compassion and contempt. A world in which you see the best and the worst in people, where you find good and bad leadership, overwhelming fatigue and inspiring resilience, and uplifting teamwork and mateship. It is a world in which survival and taking care of your mates are the real measures of success.

This is a soldiers' book, written by soldiers, in their own words. I knew many of the men commemorated in these stories and their personalities leap out of each page as though it were only yesterday. Of course, from my own recollections, a few expletives seem to have been deleted!

Major General PJ Abigail, AO
Land Commander Australia

CONTENTS

ACKNOWLEDGMENTS

This book would not have been possible without help from the veterans who walked over dead ground and lived it again. We thank them.

We also thank those who chipped in with support and encouragement—the men from Charlie Company, 3RAR—Paul 'Aub' Dwyer, Colonel Peter Scott, Alan 'AB' Pearce, Allyn McCulloch, John Wadlow, Bruce James-Martin, and Liz and Denise. A special thanks to the friends of Trevor Lynch: Wayne 'Bluey' Clarke, David Harding and Christopher Kitchenmeister—you were there when he needed you. Thanks, too, to New Holland's Publishing Manager, Anouska Good, for driving the project forward, and to Sean Doyle for another outstanding job editing one of our books.

Reference for refreshment and accuracy was taken from Mike English's excellent *The Rifleman* (Australian Military History Publications, 1999), *The RAAF in Vietnam* and *Medicine at War* (Allen & Unwin, 1994 and 1995).

BACKGROUND BRIEFING

Australia's military involvement in the Vietnam War began in May 1962. The Australian Government eventually withdrew all military forces from the conflict in 1972—the end of this country's longest war, effectively 10 years, and of a commitment which divided this nation, at times, in violent, bloody confrontation between anti-war demonstrators and authorities. Many will recall that the Vietnam experience actually led to blood being split on Australian streets.

Here is a brief chronicle of Australia's involvement in Vietnam:

- May 1962—The Australian Army Training Team, a group of 30 officers and senior NCOs, is dispatched to training installations across Vietnam.
- June 1964—The number of advisers is increased to 80. The first Australian, Warrant Officer Kevin Conway, is killed in combat in July.
- November 1964—The Australian Government introduces selective conscription.
- May 1965—1st Battalion Royal Australian Regiment and support units, totalling 1100 men, arrive at Bien Hoa and begin ground operations with the 173rd Airborne Brigade (US).
- January 1966—Prime Minster Harold Holt increases the Australian commitment to two infantry battalions, 5RAR and 6RAR, and a Task Force group—4500 men, including 500 conscripts—which arrive in South Vietnam's Phuoc Tuy Province in April 1966.
- December 1966—The Australian Government increases its commitment to the war with another infantry battalion, taking the ground force to about 6500.
- January 1968—Major Australian combat units begin operations in Bien Hoa and Long Kanh provinces.

Communists launch the TET Offensive and the Vietnam War reaches its highest level of intensity—as does opinion about it in the US and Australia.

- November 1968—President Richard Nixon pledges to end the war and negotiate an acceptable peace.
- April 1970—It is announced that one of the Task Force's infantry battalions will be withdrawn. The South Vietnamese Army takes a greater combat role in the war.
- September–October 1971—The last major actions involving Australian troops.
- November 1971—4RAR/NZ(ANZAC) is the last unit to withdraw from the Task Force base at Nui Dat.
- November 1972—A handful of Australian advisers remain in South Vietnam. All Australian troops are home by Christmas.
- March 1973—Prime Minister Gough Whitlam announces the establishment of diplomatic relations with Hanoi, while still recognising the South Vietnamese Government.
- March 1973—The last US troops leave Vietnam.
- April 1975—The Australian embassy in Saigon closes and South Vietnam continues to fight the North.
- April 1975—Ten years after Australia's involvement in the war began, South Vietnam falls to Communist forces.

THE ENEMY IN PHUOC TUY PROVINCE IN 1966–67

The North Vietnamese Army (NVAs) 274 Main Force Regiment—known as the Dong Nai Regiment—moved into Phuoc Tuy's north-western zone in 1965. It comprised two experienced battalions, totalling about 2000 soldiers. The NVA were trained, disciplined and well-armed troops with support units of mortar and heavy machine-gun squads as well as engineers, or sappers, capable of carrying out well-executed assaults on an Australian or American force of almost any size. In November

1965, the 275 Regiment ambushed and virtually wiped out an elite South Vietnamese Ranger Battalion in central Phuoc Tuy Province—only five kilometres from where the Australian Task Force would be built.

In addition, a Vietcong (VC) mobile battalion, known as D445 Provincial Mobile Battalion, with an estimated 550 soldiers, was active in the province.

All this was supported by 400 guerillas operating in groups ranging from 5 to 60 in number. These VC units were supported and directed by Vietcong infrastructure in villages and hamlets across Phuoc Tuy. During their 6 years of operations in Phuoc Tuy and Long Khan provinces, the Australians confronted a force of between 3000 and 5000 enemy, reinforced in the late 1960s by elements of the 3/33 North Vietnamese Army.

COMPOSITION OF AUSTRALIAN COMBAT UNITS

Military units referred to in this book range from section to Task Force and battalion strength. During the war no unit was up to full strength, for a variety of reasons, ranging from sickness and casualties to leave and unit transfers. But generally—on the books—the units were as follows:

- An **infantry** section comprised 10 men including a corporal in command.
- A **platoon** numbered 33 men, including the platoon sergeant. There was also a 2nd lieutenant or lieutenant in command.
- An infantry **company**, usually about 120 men, comprising three platoons and a company headquarters group and commanded by a major.
- A **battalion**—nine of which were formed and saw active service during the Vietnam War—numbered just over 800 troops, and was made up of four infantry companies (A, B, C, D),

Administration Company, Support Company, and a Battalion Headquarters Group. The Support Company included Signals, Mortars, Assault Pioneers and an Anti-Tank Platoon, which also carried out tracking and reconnaissance duties. The battalion was commanded by a lieutenant-colonel.

- A **regiment** comprised three infantry battalions and supporting services. Australia did not have a regiment at the start of its involvement in the Vietnam War, so a Task Force of two battalions and support services was assembled for service in Vietnam in 1966.

The First Australian Task Force included the two battalions (5RAR and 6RAR), artillery (1st Field Regiment), an armoured component (1st Armoured Personnel Carrier Squadron), engineers from the 1st Field Squadron, 103 Signals Squadron, 3 Squadron Special Air Services (SAS), a Task Force logistics company, and the RAAF's No. 9 Squadron of helicopters and Independent Reconnaissance Flight aircraft. The two battalions were reinforced by a third battalion in late 1967.

NATIONAL SERVICE

All 20-year-old males in Australia were required to register for National Service, or conscription. The exceptions were tribal Aborigines, non-naturalised immigrants, employees of a foreign government, and permanent members of the armed forces. There were two registration periods a year: in January for those turning 20 in the first half of the year, and in July for those with birthdays in the second half. In 1965 an annual maximum requirement of 4200 men was set; this figure was raised to 8400 a year from 1966.

Selection by ballot was adopted and conducted each March and September, with marbles representing two dates—one in the first half of the year, one in the second—drawn from a barrel. Males with those birth dates were called up. Those who did not register for conscription, about 12,000 in all, were liable to be fined and conscripted whether or not their birth dates were chosen in the ballot.

VIETNAM WAR FACTS

- Overall casualties: 5.7 million
- Estimated dead: 2.1 million
- Dustoff missions: 500,000
- Estimated South Vietnamese killed: 587,000
- South Vietnamese military killed: 220,000
- Defoliants sprayed: 19 million (US) gallons
- Helicopters used: 12,000
- Helicopters shot down: 4865
- Americans killed: 58,169
- Australians killed: 520
- Average age of Australian soldier in Vietnam: 20
- Average age of Australian soldier in World War II: 26
- Number of Australians who registered for National Service: 804,000. Of these 63,735 were called up and 19,450 went to Vietnam.
- Number of National Servicemen who became casualties: 1479, with 200 dead
- Numbers of days Australian combatants in the field in one year: 314
- Number of Australians/New Zealanders medivaced by Hercules aircraft: 3238

Phuoc Tuy Province

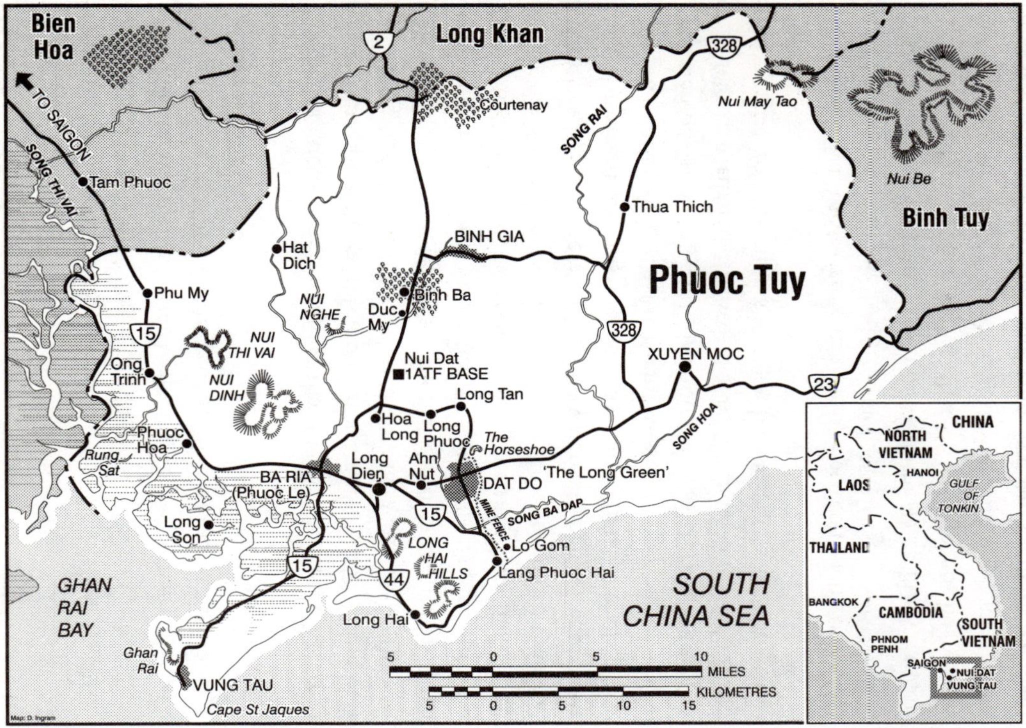

Bien Hoa
Long Khan
Binh Tuy
Phuoc Tuy
TO SAIGON
SONG THI VAI
Tam Phuoc
Courtenay
SONG RAI
Nui May Tao
Nui Be
Thua Thich
BINH GIA
Hat Dich
Phu My
Binh Ba
NUI NGHE
Duc My
NUI THI VAI
NUI DINH
Ong Trinh
Nui Dat
1ATF BASE
Long Tan
XUYEN MOC
Hoa Long
Long Phuoc
The Horseshoe
Phuoc Hoa
Rung Sat
Long Dien
Ahn Nut
BA RIA (Phuoc Le)
DAT DO
'The Long Green'
SONG HOA
SONG BA DAP
MINE FENCE
Long Son
LONG HAI HILLS
Lo Gom
Lang Phuoc Hai
GHAN RAI BAY
SOUTH CHINA SEA
Long Hai
Ghan Rai
VUNG TAU
Cape St Jaques
MILES
KILOMETRES
Map: D. Ingram
CHINA
NORTH VIETNAM
HANOI
GULF OF TONKIN
LAOS
THAILAND
BANGKOK
CAMBODIA
SOUTH VIETNAM
PHNOM PENH
SAIGON
NUI DAT
VUNG TAU

PROLOGUE

Names … names drift back through the smoke and rain … Wilf, Alan, Jimmy, Ted, 'Patto', Trevor, Colin …

We knew these names before Vietnam. We spent time with them during the war. And we nurtured each other in the aftermath.

That's what soldiers do.

It is the unique nature of conflict that each combatant takes from it something he will own; remember always. A Good Thing or a Bad Thing. It may be a fragment that lasts a few minutes—the sun filtering through rubber trees, a monsoonal downpour that turns everything around you into a fog; the *Time-Life*-like picture of a Vietnamese girl standing beside a road, a naked baby held high on her hip. Or it may be an image that lasted no more than the blink of an eye, a camera flash—like when the man to your front stepped forward and his footfall brought a metallic click. Next moment a lethal orange flash, then blackness.

Remember, too, a sky full of choppers, a clattering confusion of Hueys that turned the world into a brown-out of dust and stinging grit. You see men shouting, but hear only the chopping of blades.

There also was the sharing and caring between men. And there was shared grief, pain and loss.

One more vision we all carried through the years after Vietnam: The Look. Every soldier had it, the totally shagged, burnt-out, haunted stare he carried for every stinking day in a country that ground you down physically and wore you out mentally. Vietnam sucked out your life force and chewed away your nerves like an angle-grinder. All the other bits, you can't really remember because you were too bushed to give a stuff.

That's what soldiers felt.

John Steinbeck—Pulitzer Prize-winning author and World War II correspondent—mused on what men recall of war. He wrote in *Once There Was A War*:

'But do you know it, do you remember it, the drives, the attitudes, the terrors, and yes, the joys? I wonder how many men who were there remember very much ...'

As Steinbeck wrote about his war—The Big One—we write now about our war, The Long One. What sort of war was Vietnam? It was bitter, divisive, hi-tech, primitive, a mixture of rock and roll, Coca-Cola, pattern bombing, defoliants, booby-traps and body counts. It ended the lives of 5.7 million people—including 58,000 American troops and 520 Australians. Even 30 years on, it comes back to those who fought there in memories and dreams. Memories by day, dreams by night—dreams that are wide-screen productions, full colour and in stereo sound. You can reach up to that big screen and touch the images of the men who come and revisit you at night. You sometimes hear the words—during a break on a jungle track: 'Gimme a smoke, for Chrissake gimme a smoke.' Or seconds after a booby-trap has exploded: 'Are you okay? Speak to me! Are you okay?'

Those men's faces had expressions that changed as quickly as wind moves sand—from a grin to a grimace, from anguish to desperation and determination. Sometimes a glazed expression, then nothing. At other times there was humour in their faces, contempt for the misery. Australian larrikinism thrived in the war zone; diggers could find a joke in a cardiac arrest.

With time, images of things past can evaporate: there's a built-in fog machine that makes bad things go away. Not always, though. There are times when a trigger—a smell, a word spoken, a song, a whisper—puts us back in the zapped-out zone. For a freezing instant there is even terror.

That's what soldiers see.

This is the flashback, a landscape many combat veterans inhabit periodically for a minute or an hour—like they've stepped through the mirror, glanced at a repulsive vision, and recoiled. Some flashbacks have lasted since the day the events occurred; those events have never ended.

And there were those who were wounded—physically, with shattered legs, arms, both eyes taken from them. And mentally, some so deeply wounded they could no longer function. Many copped both the physical and the psychological wounds, a double blow.

War scars the individual so deeply, he can remain trapped for years until ending the pain by his own hand. And although it is difficult to believe there are worse things than being killed in war, there are those who will assure you that indeed there are.

After the body bags are counted, the real cost of battle comes silently, in the aftermath. And, if in the form of a flashback, it is both revealing and blinding. This is a story about men we knew who served, suffered, lived and died during and since the Vietnam War. They went away young and idealistic, and were touched by fire. Today, many endure the instant replay of Vietnam. We can tell their story because we were part of it … and we have our own flashbacks, too.

That's what soldiers feel.

The events in this story occurred during tours of duty between 1966 and 1972. They are not written in chronological order, as the main players were with units separated in some cases by two years or more. Parts of the book, for instance, are set in the Long Hais in 1966; others in the northern parts of Phuoc Tuy province in 1972.

The Australian units involved were 2RAR/NZ(ANZAC), 5RAR, 4RAR/NZ(ANZAC) and 3RAR, the battalions the authors served with. We knew each man mentioned in this book—trained in Australia or served in Vietnam with them as friends and soldiers. We have written their stories simply because they were diggers who served and suffered, and they embody the true character of the Anzac. We have avoided the dry analysis of the historian, the whys and wherefores of the war. The stories are told from the ground level—grunt level—and they tell of larrikins who were called to serve, inspired by their fathers and their fathers' fathers, who went to war and did their duty. The sons discovered in Vietnam that there were a few things their fathers never told them about the true nature of warfare.

The attitudes expressed in this book by Australian soldiers towards the enemy in no way reflect the attitudes they held towards the gentle and loving people of South Vietnam.

WELCOME TO THE BEAR PIT

Wilf Matusch sat at the cafe table overlooking the rolling surf at Greenmount Beach. This spot on the Queensland–New South Wales border was his favourite coffee stop. It soothed the soul, warmed the skin and gave a feeling of wellbeing. And the cappuccinos were shit-hot.

It was 7 a.m. Matusch sipped his coffee and fidgeted at his mobile phone with a sense of urgency and anticipation. He frequently leaned forward to glance up and down Marine Parade. He was looking for Shorty, shifting his eyes left then right. More fidgeting. What do you say to a man you haven't seen for 30 years? 'You're bloody late!'?

Do you think he'll turn up? He said he would on the phone, and that was why Matusch had the mobile sitting on the table; they had exchanged numbers in case of a stuff-up. But there was always that other factor when it came to veterans: the all-too-frequent no-show. You make up your mind to front, then your brain caves in and you can't walk out of the house; can't leave your peri-meter. Panic attacks, sweat without heat, then back to sitting in the chair, staring at the wall or the TV.

It was more than 30 years since Matusch had seen Shorty Mawer, and he could still clearly recall the day and the hour when he'd last glimpsed the look on the face of the patrol's forward scout.

Flashback: Wilf Matusch—Down on my knees, body forward like a Muslim praying. There's a sound close by like a water bottle being emptied on the ground. *Splat, splish, splosh.* Lean back on my legs and still the bottle splashes its contents on the ground next to me. Look around. It's not water—it's blood! Blood gushing from a hole just below my eye socket.

Vision is blurring.

Later, different sounds, different images. The dustoff chopper hovers with a clatter overhead and I'm going up through the trees, whipping under the helicopter downwash. I'm clinging to a jungle penetrator being pulled up on a winch. Below, Shorty and Bolsty are staring up at me. It's carnage down there, like the floor of an old outback slaughterhouse.

Long Khan province, South Vietnam, three months in-country. August 8, 1970, 15.30hrs, and eleven men from a 28-man platoon have been wounded by a massive Vietcong booby-trap.

Thirty years on, and there is an ache to know. What happened to the others, the rest of the men on the ground during the worst hours of their lives? What happened to Shorty after he exchanged one last look with Matusch? The guilt of the survivor: *I'm out. I've got a hole in me, but I'm out and you're still down there dealing with all that crap.*

A few minutes later at Greenmount Beach, Shorty Mawer comes into view ...

Swing west off the Gold Coast Highway near Oxenford and push up into the Darling Range. Depending how hard you're driving, you might reach Canungra in an hour. Watch the roads here— they can be a tortuous, treacherous series of twisting turns, accidents waiting to happen. Canungra has an impact on a driver akin to a bug hitting the windscreen: a backwater Dullsville in the hinterland above the Surfers Paradise sun, fun and surf strip. It's mainly forest and open paddock here in the high country, punctuated by a series of spectacular ranges. The town itself is a cluster of houses, a police station, corner shop, hotel and RSL hall.

The cemetery is beside the road that ascends the final hill to the entrance of what was once the Jungle Training Centre—'JTC' to its 'friends'. Stop the car a minute and recall, years back, when JTC staff member, Lance-Corporal 'Massa' Clarke, and his mates got so drunk at the pub that when they left to stagger back to the barracks, they wandered off the road and fell asleep among the gravestones. God knows what 'Massa' thought when he woke, startled from his semi-comatose state that morning, but to the Torres Strait Islander it must have seemed like he had joined his ancestors. Some of those present claim Massa actually turned pale that morning.

From the front gate of the JTC, drive up the main road and the first building you sight is the HQ. Wind to your right slightly past the flagpoles—there are the old cinema and the Regimental Aid Post. Next, pass the Officers' and Sergeants' messes, buildings still recognisable today despite refurbishment and additions. Looking across the valley, you see Battle Wing in the distance. You drive past the long, double-storey accommodation blocks where the sergeant instructors and the Demonstration Company diggers used to collapse after humping around the hilly terrain all day long.

Next, the family store and main canteen alongside the barber shop, where a long-haired, droopy-moustached civilian named Peter lent interest-free cash to soldiers who were a bit short at the end of the week. Peter was highly thought of at JTC, for not only was he a good barber, money lender and nice bloke, he was also an honorary member of the Sergeants' Mess, and liked to have a beer with all the members.

Down along the thickly-vegetated, lantana-covered creek line—on the opposite side of the road to the canteen—is the Confidence Course. Seeing this again after so many years causes the heart to race and the temples to pound; this is where men's pain barometers burst.

Drive on slowly, and it becomes apparent that the centre has changed in 20 years. But curiously, the old Battle Wing HQ on

Battle Ridge is caught in a time warp: except for the dust and cobwebs on the windows and the faded paintwork on the old wooden buildings, nothing's really changed at all. The Army closed down the jungle training aspects of the centre long ago and has since given the place an extensive update—long overdue, as it was originally constructed during World War II. The Land Warfare Centre, as it is called today, may have a new training focus and identity, but to some of us it will always be JTC. Despite the manicured lawns and new red-brick buildings, it remains in the minds of thousands of battle-hardened veterans a place where young men's bones, hearts and spirits were either galvanised or broken.

In the 1960s and '70s, Canungra was a pit of pain. Up in the hinterland it was a sauna by day, where thousands of troops struggled through the mud and lantana. And by night, as the long shadows of darkness crept over the Centre and the sun dropped behind Mt Tamborine, the mist and cold forced men to seek warmer clothing. The water in the fire buckets often turned to ice. You imagined freezing to death in the jungle, teeth chattering, curled up in the foetal position in a futile attempt to preserve body heat.

Every man that lived in the shadow of a posting to South Vietnam 'did Canungra'. It was a three-week, highly intensive battle indoctrination course where cooks, engineers, medics, administration staff, drivers and riflemen were dragged by the scruff of the neck through the mud, the blood and the beer. Everyone who ever went through JTC got a condensed version of life as seen through the sweat-impaired vision of the grunt.

What burned JTC into the mind was a combination of the rough jungle environment, exhaustion, and the men who ran it— a mixed bag of military legends, heroes and bastards whose spirits still haunt the place. Close your eyes, you can hear and see them. Hungarian-born Major Felix 'The Cat' Fazekas, MC, was one such legend. 'The Cat' had fled communist Hungary with a price on his head and joined the Australian Army. He loved all things military, coveted command, and embraced the Aussie traditions—but he never truly mastered the lingo.

'Vot da blue fuck do you think you're doing, dickhead?' only brought chortles and grins from all except whoever he was berating. He was the master of the mutant metaphor: 'Ven da cat is away the mice vill dance, eh?' he sniggered after learning that some junior officers had trashed the Officers' Mess in his absence.

JTC was also home to Warrant Officer Instructor (WO2) Allen 'Clackers' Clutterbuck. Looking into his dinner plate-sized eyes, you'd swear the man was either hypnotised or mad. Then there was the 'Grey Ghost', Laurie Mooney, who had the complexion of a corpse. Mooney could often be seen standing in a corner of the bar, staring into oblivion. He rarely spoke … just stared. 'Ozzie' Ostara, DCM, was the Regimental Sergeant Major. What he lacked in height he made up for in leadership and soldiering ability. He drank with the hirsute Garry Chad, a sergeant whose favourite party trick was to set fire to his chest hair. 'Grub' McGrath, Mentioned in Dispatches for courage during his time with the Australian Army Training Team in Vietnam, called everyone 'cobber' and had a squint in one eye. His simple bushy look and demeanour were enhanced by the roll-your-own cigarette that dangled from his bottom lip every waking hour. When you looked into Grub's unsquinting eye, you also wondered what it was about the man that made him a Scrabble champion.

These men had become legends in relatively recent times. Others had enjoyed a stellar status for far longer when they joined the training staff to teach the art of war. These included 'Bomber' Harris, a tail-gunner on an aircraft in the squadron that flew the famous Dambuster missions in World War II, when British bomber pilots destroyed the Germans' Ruhr dam with special bouncing bombs. And there was WO Bill Tillett, also a World War II veteran. Fit, but slower than most, Tillett was the oldest and one of the most experienced instructors at Canungra.

Everyone at JTC had a moniker: Noel 'Mad Dog' Smith, Lt Colonel 'Rotten' Ron Grey, Colonel Jimmy 'Hooky' Hughes, Major Barry 'Tigerman' Peterson, WO Joe 'Mechanical Mouse' Joyce. They were legends then, today they're memories.

Among the thousands who passed through JTC before embarkation were Infantrymen Trevor Lynch, Wilf Matusch, Colin Cogswell, Jimmy Griffiths, Dave Paterson, Alan Dwyer and Ted Harrison—faces in the crowd, ordinary young blokes, National Servicemen and Regular Army diggers who considered service in the Army to be a spot of adventure, maybe even a career. They'd heard of Vietnam, even heard of the war there, but few could find it on a map.

Dave 'Patto' Paterson was a second lieutenant. Your first impression of him was his size—he topped six feet, six inches, and his boots were specially handmade to fit his size-15 feet. He was a gentle giant, a family man who spoke lovingly of a wife and baby daughter and regularly attended church services.

JTC brought every man, commissioned officer or baggy-arsed grunt, back to basics. After early morning runs along broken, dusty tracks as the day's 'warm-up', each soldier pulled on his basic webbing—bum-pack, belt, ammunition pouches and water bottles—and fastened a sling onto his self-loading rifle.

Lined up with their platoon, the men were briefed by a sergeant on what could be expected on the Confidence Course. This instructor was a hard little bastard who had long ago been branded 'the Gnome'. He double-timed the platoon up the hill to the starting point, where each man prepared himself mentally for the toughest fifteen minutes of his life. The Gnome instructed the platoon to break into groups of three so they could set off at a run two minutes apart. He was hitting his straps, almost frothing. 'Don't fuck around waiting for your mates, this is an individual effort—and it's timed. Go!'

Flashback: Jimmy Griffiths—Sweating like a racehorse and haven't even bloody started yet. The other two blokes shoot forward. Gotta get in front of those two or I'll be held up at one of the obstacles.

Boom! Boom!

Shit, they're throwing thunder flashes at the men in front— simulated grenade explosions that'd blow the eardrums out, I reckon. First obstacle coming up and the friggin' rifle is slapping against my back and the water bottles on the belt are chewing into my hips. Three narrow poles set horizontally across a muddy creek. Try to balance and walk over but the new combat boots and their rubber soles slip and I plunge down. Freezing splash and crawl out onto the bank, ready to go again.

'Where the fuck you goin', dickhead? Get up and do it properly.' Quick look at the instructor. Wanna shoot the prick.

Now there's a *pop* and *whoosh* as smoke grenades are tossed at us. Yellow, red and green gaseous clouds drift across the course and instantly I'm spitting up lumps of clag I never knew were in my body. Can't breathe properly. Now there are three horizontal pipes ahead. I recall being told to go through backwards or I'll exit face-first to another stinking waterhole.

Crack, crack, crack. An M60 machine-gun opens up with blanks. More ear-popping, but now another hassle—the bloody rifle sling has wrapped around my throat. Can't breathe again.

Look behind while running towards the hanging rope: I'm in front of the other two in my trio and they're bitching at each other to get out of the way. *Stay in front, must stay in front.* Jump for the rope hanging over the moat—and realise I'm not going to make it. Soaked clothes and saturated webbing drag me down, and the burning sensation in my hands is unbearable.

Splash.

Now my boots are sinking into mud. I'm gonna die.

'Move! Come on, keep movin'! It's the Gnome, and there's a look of pleasure on the mongrel's face. I must look like The Creature From The Black Lagoon—encased in mud, water sluicing down my neck, staggering towards the next hell.

The wall is 8 feet high. Up and over, but the combat boots let me down again and I smash headfirst into the logs. More water and mud, and now blood running from my nose. Up and over, and for a moment I'm sitting high on top of the wall.

'Not low enough, shithead. Do that in Vietnam you'll get a third eye. I shit you not, digger.' The instructor's not happy. Fuck him.

On to the low wire entanglement. Oxygen, need more oxygen. Why not drop out? Say I've hurt myself. Can't do that, every other prick will put shit on me. Reach the bastard wire entanglement and now it's hop, skip and jump like a kid playing hopscotch across the zigzag of fixed wire strands. My trousers snag and over I go, down headfirst. More pain.

I've gained more ground on the other two. How many more minutes to go? Should do it in fifteen minutes. Some fucker did it in eleven. There's a ladder ahead that takes me up to a cable crossing. Up the ladder and the lungs are screaming for air. Grab the top cable and slide my feet out on to the slacker bottom cable. Edge out over the creek 15 feet below. Look down and I want to vomit, shit my pants, but instead I have a quick dry retch—there's even smoke from the grenades up here. Down the ladder on the other side and crawl onto my guts under the cargo net draped over a huge mud pool. The friggin' rifle snags on the net while I'm making my way like a snake through the slop.

'Speed, speed, get some more speed up. C'mon man, get all your shit in one sock, for fuck's sake.'

Some bastard's yelling again, but I don't give a toss. My throat's on fire, I've got to drink. I recall that ahead is the Bear Pit. Everyone talks about the Bear Pit and it's now in sight and I'm going to get my boots on the wall right this time. Hell, it's only a 6-foot wall. Up and over, right? I swing over the log wall. Hell, I'm in a friggin' void! Then *splat* and a whole new world of shit.

The pit is a stagnant soup of coal-black slime and before I can close my mouth, it gurgles down inside me. I have to puke. Crawl out and slide back, crawl and slide again, then at last back on my feet. How many minutes to go? Am I gonna beat the clock? There's a slopping sound behind me, punctuated by a curse. The others are catching up. I reach the vertical cargo net, swing aboard and begin the climb. There's no power left in my arms; I hang suspended. Every atom of muscle is now screaming *stop*. After the cargo net, the mind goes blank and I switch to autopilot as I slop in boots full of water across a bitumen road. There's a Land-Rover coming, making its way to the main gate. Hit me. Hit me now and I'll go to hospital and a nice bed.

Now over the wobble boards and then up onto the rope and the car-tyre obstacle. Hang onto the rope and keep my footing on the rubber tyres because there's more water below. Fall, and it'll be up and do it again. Can just hear the machine-gun still firing, but the smoke's gone. Thank you, God. Ahead, climbing 30 feet into the air, is The Tower. There's an instructor on top and in the river below a boat and three men wearing diving gear—wetsuits, snorkels and flippers.

'Come on. Get up. It's not a playground!' I drag myself up. The instructor at the top of the platform quickly checks me, checks that my pockets are inside out, and nudges me forward.

'Swimmer or non-swimmer?' He grins. 'S'easy, put your arms out, look straight ahead. Shit, even the padre floated and you know how holy he is. You end up at the bottom in the mud and we'll send the divers in.'

I spreadeagle like a man ready for crucifixion and step off ...

Minutes later, soaked and freezing, hands resting on knees, I'm standing near two instructors, Vietnam veterans who are carefully watching me for any reaction.

A soldier, still gasping from the Course, grunts: 'Can't tell me we gotta do any shit like that in Vietnam?'

The two instructors say nothing. There's a secret shared as the two vets look at each other almost sympathetically, and quietly walk away.

BLOODING

Vietnam appeared in the briefing pamphlet as a narrow strip stuck on the eastern side of the Indochina Peninsula as an afterthought. One land, two countries: The South and the Communist North fighting for the unification of the two peoples.

Always keep it basic for the grunt: simplistic, digestible bites of information was the soldiers' diet. It had to be—we didn't want philosophical thought or political debate in the middle of a fire-fight. So the idea was to train the combatant so he was drilled in protocols and techniques on how to fight—not how to think. For this reason, a simple brochure on the history of the country, its people and culture had been prepared; a sort of Cook's Tour Of The War Zone. The leaflet told how the people of the former French colony had endured many years of war. They were a courteous, religious people and should be treated as such. Soldiers in other wars had probably had their version of the brochure, which said nothing about dirty politics, crises or commitments.

One week in-country, and it was time for a reality check. The brochure was right on one score: these people had long endured war. They had been bombed, burnt, abused, tortured, raped, oppressed, imprisoned and generally head-kicked by a succession of regimes. Indochina in the '60s was not on most people's tourist itinerary.

The Cook's Tour never mentioned the Bad Things: the disease, the blood-sucking bugs and the fact that this conflict had no frontline. War surrounded you in Vietnam no matter where you operated. There was also a reference to Dry and Wet seasons; Vietnam was monsoonal. Many diggers thought monsoons had something to do with the moon. Reality check again: monsoon means rain. Not just showers, but torrential downpours that lasted for hours and almost beat you to death.

Country life: the buildings varied from old French villas—

some honeycombed with bullet holes—in shaded gardens to compressed kerosene-can hootchies and thatched huts. The archetypal rural scene was a water buffalo with a young boy astride it while mamasan and papasan beat the beast through water-filled rice padis. It was Third World and peaceful, a place of conical hats, pigs and coopfuls of chickens riding on top of buses and Lamborettas.

Saigon was an ocean of old Renaults and Citroens, tricycles and beautiful women on bicycles who wore the traditional 'Au Dai' skirt, with a slit up the side that made your tongue hang out. The backstreets brimmed with rotting vegetables and fish, whose stench encouraged breathing out, not in. Saigon was yahoo-ing Yanks with cameras, boozed-up Aussies on Rest and Convalescence, Vietnamese soldiers on the hustle, and the 'White Mice', Vietnamese police—resentful, mean-spirited, hand resting on a loaded .45. The kids smoked Salems, the bar-girls swilled Saigon Tea and the soldiers drank a local brew called 'Barmy Ba 33'. It was hostile territory, running on nerves, profiteering and booze.

Like out in the 'weeds'—the 'J', the 'sticks', the jungle: all hostile and all nerves, all day.

Three months in-country, and Colin Cogswell was already living on his nerves. The forward scout supported his Armalite with one arm and used the other to manipulate the 'ghost stick' while he walked. The ghost stick was a sapling he held in one hand, dangling downwards, that would touch a booby-trap's fishing line-thick twine, connected to the grenade, before he put his size-9 boot into it. It takes 20 pounds of pressure to set off a trip wire—one of the smaller details Cogswell had wised up to in

Vietnam. He hoped he would detect in his fingers the slightest pressure against the sapling as it touched wire.

Lead scout for 5 Section, 5 Platoon, Cogswell was sweating as much through the exertion of lugging a load up a mountain infested with Vietcong as he was over the fact that further down the slopes another rifle company was still extracting its wounded from a booby-trap detonation. Section commander Jimmy Hall had warned his scout with a whispered, 'Nice and slow, watch every step.' Cogswell hardly had to be reminded about how carefully to move: he'd be the first to hear the click and the first to be taken out if he snagged a trip wire.

The topography on the Nui Thi Vai Mountains changed constantly. Cogswell carefully negotiated a narrow gully and began to lead the section of Australian Infantry up a sharper ravine. Here, thick bush gave away to huge boulders and organ pipe-shaped fingers of granite. He stopped behind a boulder for a breather, and took a slug from his water bottle. The section's second scout, Doug, stopped further down the gully and waited for him to move on.

Cogswell always wanted to be at the sharp end of things, a grunt out front. The young soldier had dreamed since childhood of a life in the military. Born in Britain and migrating to Australia in 1956, his world rapidly became a series of boys' homes after his parents separated. Life on the move, a nomadic transfer from one home to another for nearly four years, hardened the youngster. He took a full-time job at 13, as a storeman's assistant in a welding factory. But he dreamed Army. He lied about his age and tried to get in at 15½, but was easily spotted in the Recruiting Centre for failing to produce his birth certificate. He went back at 17 and immediately signed up for six years. He would have signed for life. He wanted to be a soldier and he wanted Infantry. After recruit training, he was slotted for engineering. Cogswell argued for and was eventually given Infantry because he'd been quickly slated as a marksman on the rifle range.

Still too young for active service after completing Infantry training, he cooled his heels at Ingleburn's Infantry Training Centre with Demonstration Platoon. Then, the week he turned 19, he scored a spare seat on a 707 and headed for the action.

Back on the mountain, he took a deep breath and prepared to move ahead.

Flashback: Colin Cogswell—The smell behind the boulder is pungent; the odour of another race. Crane forward, peer around the rock, scarcely able to breathe. A Vietcong commander is standing less than eight feet from me! It's like a picture in some magazine of Mao Tse Tung—baggy caps, khaki uniforms, and there are so bloody many! Maybe I should count them? Don't be a bloody idiot.

One man stands out—the commander. He's got a presence about him, and there's a red star on the front of his cap. So close … so close I could butt-stroke him with my rifle. Heart thumping like a hammer in my chest. Mouth turning dry and arsehole clenching.

The smell! Jeepers, they must be able to smell me, too. Vietcong? More likely North Vietnamese Regular soldiers, hardcore—and they're going through a briefing. Every enemy soldier is focused on the urgent instructions from the commander. Must be getting ready to piss off, and I'm feeling as obvious as a third nostril.

Slump back behind the boulder and peer down the hill for Doug. No Doug—bugger's bolted off to alert the platoon commander that we're up against a shit-load of Nogs. What if a Nog comes around the rock to have a quiet piss? I'll move to the other end of the boulder …

Shit! High above are caves, more enemy. Squat quietly and try to control my breathing. Where the hell is the rest of the platoon? Look at my watch—45 minutes I've been stuck here. I can see machine-gunner Joe Devlin move into position. We're not going to assault this mob, surely not. Doug is signalling now to get back. Thank fuck!

Cogswell scrambled back to his section. Minutes later, the mountainside erupted in a sickly flash of orange and black smoke. The detonations of napalm from the American F100 Phantoms were followed by raking cannon fire. Then the first barrage of heavy artillery came in like a freight train.

The caves of Nui Thi Vai had been occupied by the 274 Regiment of the North Vietnamese Army; enemy heavyweights under its Deputy Commander Nguyen Nam Hung. The Australian forces in Phuoc Tuy usually didn't give a hoot who was commanding the opposition, but Nguyen Nam Hung was known as a hard case. He was in Phuoc Tuy to kick Aussie arse, and he had the numbers to do it. His troops were trained to fight and hold ground—particularly in the Nui Thi Vais—and they had the weaponry. The Nuis—or the 'Warbies', as the Australians called them—comprised jungle, vines and boulders the size of the one Cogswell had squatted behind when he spotted the large force. The mountain was a cobweb of tripwires and landmines. A patrol up here was bad news; an attack meant woundings and death.

Better to bring in heavy firepower. Vietnam warfare was all about armament and ordnance. From the air it was 500- or 1000-pound bombs, and the horrific jelly-flame of napalm that sucked the oxygen from the air and incinerated the enemy. On the ground it was cannister and splintex that shredded the jungle and anyone in it with darts of flechette or hundreds of ball-bearings fired from a tank, an artillery piece or even a special Infantryman's weapon. This was how the Allied Forces were going to win the war: bomb the suitcases out of every inch of the country and blow every enemy soldier into next week. But this was where somebody had a serious lapse of judgment and foresight—the Vietcong had seen it all before; they had endured, they had survived and they were in for the long haul.

One of Charlie's standard tactics was the 'suck in'—pull the opposition onto his ground and kill him by any means. On Nui Thi Vai and its sister peak, Nui Toc Tien, the NVA had burrowed into the rock and established a cave and bunker network. They had also strung booby-traps and anti-personnel mines in the path of advancing troops. The Australian advance into this mountainous hideout began at 3 a.m. with C Company, 5th Battalion moving over the southern slopes into an area of operation called 'Christine'. (The Army had a strange predeliction for naming operational areas and fire support bases after its commanders' wives.)

On the peak above Cogswell, 5th Battalion's Assault Pioneers moved up to begin their work. The area had been bombed and chopped up in an airstrike, but mines and booby-traps were still active in and around the caves. Assault Pioneers, Infantry-style engineers, are trained to detect and blow mines. But Platoon Commander John Macaloney was also up here to clear the caves with flame-throwers—nasty work in any grunt's book. Any digger who had seen World War II movies of Americans assaulting the islands in the Pacific campaign and winkling the Japanese out of caves with long bursts of flame, was now going to get a taste of the real thing on the Warbies.

Assault Pioneer Trevor Lynch was with the flame-throwing party. He squatted, waiting while Macaloney approached the cave entrance with a man in escort. Lynch hunkered down with his rifle at the ready and scanned the high ground. From his position, the rifleman could keep an eye on the Pioneer group carrying the flame-throwers—men with tanks of petroleum mixture on their backs that fed into a nozzle. An igniter in the nozzle would set the mixture on fire as it shot out. Lynch noticed the platoon commander station a digger near the tunnel entrance. Inside the narrow cave, Macaloney first detected the smell of the enemy, then saw the booby-trap and its triggering device. He bent to examine it.

Crack!

A rifle shot rang out behind him. Macaloney scrambled out of the cave, calling to the digger on sentry to take cover. Another *crack*—the soldier spun and dropped to the ground. Macaloney screamed to his machine-gunner to cut loose on the Vietcong sniper. Granite fragmented, bullets ricocheted and the gullys reverberated to the deafening sounds of the firefight. The sniper suddenly showed his head. *Crack!* He was felled by a single shot from a section commander. Ricochets were the greatest hazard during a firefight in rocky terrain: bullets were rattling around the rocks, sending knife-sharp chips of granite flying at the soldiers. One ricochet hit Macaloney and tore flesh away from the side of his head.

Flashback: Trevor Lynch—Shit! A digger's been hit by a sniper. Move up, got to move up. Scrambling, staggering ... bush and boulders everywhere. Rifle up and start shooting, pouring a wall of fire into and around the cave. Macaloney's tossing grenades into the cave entrance, more automatic fire—Macaloney's gone down, hit by a ricochet. I'm up with the flame-thrower party ...

moving. Can see the first searing tongue of fuel shoot forward into the cave's blackness. I'm slipping behind the main group. Log ahead. Bend and get under, quick.

A sudden flash of orange and blackness. Someone snagged a booby-trap wire and Lynch took the full impact of the explosion. The blast ripped through the front of his body, breaking both legs and shredding his face.

THE FUNNY FARM

There were several ways to get a soldier to war. You could put him on a ship, as they did in World Wars I and II; stinking, fart-filled vessels where soldiers squeezed into hammocks and lay around on deck, sweating off being torpedoed by a German sub.

The situation for the digger on his way to Vietnam was not quite so primitive, and there was no danger of being sunk. Under the rotation system—whereby a fresh battalion of 800 replaced another that had completed its twelve-month tour of duty—many of the soldiers were transported to and from the war zone aboard the HMAS *Sydney*, a refitted aircraft carrier, later dubbed the 'Vung Tau Ferry'. On board, men trained, exercised, boxed and shot at coloured balloons released over the water. They slept in hammocks, and the food was adequate and plentiful.

Each of the relieving battalions sent an Advance Party by Qantas 707, which included senior officers to be briefed by their departing counterparts. Groups of soldiers and non-commissioned officers went ahead with the Advance Party, for administration purposes and to begin relieving the troops in the field. The 707 was usually drunk dry by the time it reached Singapore, where the soldiers disembarked—in civilian clothing—for a brief stop. This was cloak-and-dagger stuff: the Singaporeans weren't supposed to know the Australians were taking a refuelling stop in their country on the way to war.

Flashback: Colin Cogswell—What a bloody joke this is. Sure, no Army uniform, but 100 blokes walking across the tarmac all wearing shiny black shoes, polyester khaki trousers held up with a thin khaki web belt, and all wearing a white civvy shirt. Lee Kwan Yew obviously mustn't realise that anyone with an IQ higher than a retarded orangutan's couldn't see at a casual glance that we're soldiers. If the Singaporeans are still stuck as to the nationality of this bunch, just have a listen in—'Bloody plane's out of piss before we reach Darwin. Now the fuckin' airport bar's closed. What kind of rinky-dink war are the bastards sendin' us to?'

The Advance Party on the chartered jet landed at Tan Son Nhut airport in Saigon, at the time the busiest airport in the world. The air here was fetid with heat, the smell of aircraft fuel and the stench of rotting vegetables that pervaded Vietnam. The sign on the terminal read: 'WELCOME TO SAIGON—THE PARIS OF THE ORIENT.' Maybe there was a similarity between the stink and rubbish here and the smells and garbage in the French capital. Maybe over there they had a sign reading 'Welcome to Paris—The Saigon of Europe'. Maybe that's why Paris was hosting the peace talks to stop the war. The air around Tan Son Nhut was so putrid, you imagined you could put it between two slices of bread and make a sandwich. A shit sandwich.

The war was all about air power and air mobility; at some stage everyone flew, either hanging out of an Iroquois helicopter, wobbling about in the back of a Caribou, or cold and half-deafened in the much larger C130 Hercules. Coming in on Advance Parties were Wilf Matusch, Lt Dave Paterson and Alan 'Doggy' Dwyer—three men who had found their way to the war at different times and through different choices. Like every soldier at the beginning of their tour of duty, they got their first taste—or smell—of Asia.

And they headed for the Big Red Rat: Nui Dat, Vietnamese for 'small hill', and the location of the First Australian Task Force (1ATF). Home to nearly 2000 Australians by the late 1960s, it was a self-contained city of tents, iron sheds and workshops, artillery gun positions and daily convoys of trucks hauling supplies from the seaport of Vung Tau, 30 kilometres south on the Cape St Jacques. Those trucks had a red kangaroo stencilled on the doors, which to the Vietnamese and most Americans looked like a large hopping rodent—hence the 'Big Red Rat'. HMAS *Sydney* stood offshore in the South China Sea while giant twin-rotored Chinook helicopters ferried the men to Nui Dat.

Alan 'Doggy' Dwyer was chuffed he'd landed in the war. He was a part-country boy from Badgery's Creek outside Sydney, and he was destined to be the company clown—trouble in uniform, with a shock of blond hair and a half-moon grin. With his hands shoved deep in his pockets, he was the military version of Charlie Chaplin. He wanted to be in the Army; the life suited him. He particularly liked the mateship, which provided him with a ready audience. He loved Army procedure and its inflexible regimentation because it gave him continual ammunition for a biting sense of humour second to none.

His first 'funny' in-country was on the flight from Saigon to Nui Dat. He feigned amazement at how the Vietnamese farmers had such 'sound agricultural techniques', like saving water in the thousand dams he could see below. It was a great idea, chortled Dwyer to his mates, who had a perplexed look on their faces. He waffled on until a soldier coming back to the war zone on his second tour took the bait. 'They're not dams, they're bomb craters with water in 'em, you bloody idiot.'

Dwyer put on his best shocked expression, then the moon-sized grin. Two days later, the grin was gone.

The 19-year-old digger's boots had hardly picked up the red mud around the tents at Nui Dat when a soldier departing for home after a year in-country threw him a special 30-round magazine for his Armalite rifle. The soldier then tossed him a set of American Special Forces camouflage greens.

'You sure you don't need them any more?' Dwyer asked.

The soldier walked away from the tent, cackling, 'You'll be sorry.'

Dwyer, a green forward scout, slipped off his 20-round magazine and slammed on the curved 30-rounder, and with his tiger-pattern shirt and trousers he felt he was now in a war for sure.

I'm ready to close with and kill the enemy.

Five minutes later, another soldier stuck his head in the tent. 'You Dwyer, the new guy? Get up to the Quartermaster and grab an M60—you're going on patrol.'

Dwyer sat and looked at the Armalite rifle he had been issued that morning—then called out to the soldier who was disappearing between rows of tents, 'I'm a scout, not a gunner.'

Three hours later, South Vietnam's newest Aussie arrival was lugging the M60 machine-gun—an Infantry section's heaviest firepower—through the huge walls of barbed wire that encircled the Task Force base. He was heading into VC territory. As each man cocked his weapon, Dwyer tried to cock the M60—unsuccessfully. He lifted and cleared the feed plate; it still wouldn't cock. He squatted, removed the link belt of ammunition, and again tried to cock it. The gun refused to feed; he just couldn't put a round 'up the spout'. By now the patrol was melting into the treeline. Dwyer pulled himself up, tossed the belts of link ammunition across his shoulder and hurried in pursuit. For two days he patrolled the jungle cursing the useless M60, too scared to breathe a word to anyone. The boy from Badgery's Creek had come to the war seeking the enemy, and was now praying he wouldn't find them.

Hours after landing at Nui Dat, Wilf Matusch sat on his cot wondering what sort of war he'd come to. He was still in his polyester uniform and black shoes, and held his slouch hat in his hands.

What made him feel more like a bacon burger in a synagogue was the fact he still didn't have a weapon. His mates, 'Sparrow' Aitken and 'Johnno' Johnson, had arrived days earlier—also part of the Advance Party—and were already stripped to the waist in jungle-green pants.

While Matusch struggled with the absurdity of his situation, Aitken lifted a steel helmet off one of the exterior tent poles and revealed a bleached-white human skull. 'I'm going to call our tent the "Skull Cave",' he chuckled.

Johnno planned to get more skulls to put on the endposts that supported the mosquito nets over each cot. 'It'll give us something to look at after we crawl into our mossie playpens,' he said with deadly seriousness. Matusch wondered how long it took to go mad in Vietnam.

A C-123 Hercules, the 'Baby Herc'—a stubby, shortened version of the big Hercules transporter—was taxiing towards Lieutenant Dave Paterson. It was an ugly, dark green piece of machinery that shuddered and whined as its engines shut down and the back ramp dropped. Two Thai pilots strolled down the ramp and looked across at the group of Australians, grinning and pointing inside the plane. This was Paterson's shuttle to Nui Dat. Two Asian pilots and the state of the plane didn't exactly instil confidence. The huge Second Lieutenant took up almost two spaces on the nylon bench seats and his legs reached across to the other side of the aircraft as he strapped in next to fellow Australian lieutenant, Bob Lewis, a Nasho officer who, after a great night on the town, almost failed to graduate from Officer Cadet School at Scheyville. Every man on board fell silent; there was a feeling of despair and imminent doom.

Flashback: Dave Paterson—This plane doesn't look like it's been serviced since the day of manufacture: every bolt and rivet looks shaken loose, the hydraulics hiss, and every so often a loud buzzer goes off. And there's that flashing red light ... Here we go ...

The take-off seemed to extend no further than a football field, then the machine was up, engines screaming and a cloud of black smoke trailing away. The wings seemed to actually flap. Shaking violently, the plane dropped in height, climbed again, then dipped and banked steeply, pushing Paterson's stomach back against his spinal column. The passengers concentrated on the sights below in a bid to take their minds off the ride. The Mekong River, speckled with sampans, snaked away to the horizon. The land was dotted with rows of thatched huts, ox-carts and old trucks, the odd burnt-out tank, then a patch-quilt of rice padis, brown and green, and water flashing in the sun. Vietnam—pastoral, peaceful and beautiful, from the air.

Soon there was a change in vegetation: the trees became jungle in thick mats of green, with thin creek lines creeping in and out of the trees like serpents. Rain-filled bomb craters winked up. Further south, pastoral lands reappeared, with small hamlets, narrow roads and dirt tracks. Instinctively, Paterson and Lewis knew this was Bad Country, crawling with Charlie. A low range of mountains, pale blue, light brown and green, rose out of the flat lands of the south. These were Nui Thi Vai, Nui Dinh and Nui Toc Tien.

The engines dropped revs; the two men felt the plane begin its descent. The red light was still flashing when the aircraft went into what felt like a nose-dive in order to avoid possible enemy ground fire. Below, extended belts of barbed wire flashed by, then machine-gun emplacements, then *thump-thump* as the Herc's wheels met the bitumen of Luscombe Field, Nui Dat.

THE SHARP END

The youngest man in 5th Battalion was Colin Cogswell, just a week past his nineteenth birthday. The second 'babe' was Edmund 'Ted' Harrison—19 years and 28 days old when he arrived in the war zone in early May, 1966. Five months later, Harrison was on Nui Thi Vai, about 6 clicks from the newly-established Task Force base. A battalion clearing operation was underway on Nui Thi Vai and Nui Toc Tien, and on the morning of October 8, C Company's 8 Platoon encountered two VC trail-watchers. The enemy soldiers fired on the platoon, causing the men to dive off the trail in search of cover. The VC had booby-trapped all the likely fire positions, and many in 8 Platoon, including the commander, were wounded. C Company later discovered a major enemy bunker complex, with a hospital and a booby-trap factory.

Meanwhile, Ted Harrison and his platoon in A Company were moving up the southern slopes of the 'Warbies'. The company's objective was to move up the largest spur line on Nui Thi Vai, then cross the saddle to Nui Toc Tien. Not only were the hills laced with booby-traps and snipers, there was also the minor issue of falling down a one-in-two incline. Every Australian on the mountain was having an anxiety attack, including Ted Harrison.

Harrison had been baptised Edmund by his father Ted in order to carry on the family tradition of an Edmund in every generation since 1845. Ted was a surprise, the first-born to Claire, who until then was sure she was infertile. Two brothers and a sister followed in quick succession.

The Harrisons lived in a two-bedroom, semi-detached house in suburban, working-class Lewisham, in Sydney's inner-west. Tough times they were in the early 1950s, but home life was nurturing: father Edmund detailed cars on the weekends for extra cash to provide the eventual mod cons—replacing the wood stove and the ice chest, and a new hand-wringer unit instead of the old wood-fire copper washing machine. After school, young Ted cleaned the chook pen; he listened to Smokey Dawson and 'Good Morning, Sir' on the radiogram on Saturday nights.

He played soldiers and held billy-cart races with his school mate, Jimmy Tonkin. The days of sword fights and billy-carts, *Rocket Man* at the movies and playing with the stick rifle were golden memories, and in desperate times you hung onto them. They were bathed in a softness, sometimes so clear you could reach out and touch them. Each year seemed to last forever.

After two years as a lube-operator in the local garage—an 'apprenticeship', he was told—the boy from Lewisham opted for a career change and followed the Harrison tradition of joining the services. Dad had been in the RAAF during World War II; Grandfather had served with 9th Division, withstanding the German seige of Tobruk; and a close uncle had been a prisoner of war after the fall of Singapore. Ted wanted in. His dad, believing a young man should have a trade, said no. Ted persisted, wearing Mum down until she signed the application form.

His trip to Vietnam was memorable, spending most of the flight in the toilet with chronic diarrhoea. The second leg was just as exciting. Boarding the Baby Herc flight from Saigon to Vung Tau—in early 1966 Nui Dat was yet to be established—Harrison noticed oil leaking from the port engine. 'What if we run out of oil?' he asked.

The crew chief made a whistling sound and a spiralling motion downwards with his hand. 'It's okay, we'll get there—one way or another.'

Back on the Warbies, the 19-year-old felt he was sweating out a year of his life every day. The platoon forward scout indicated a track: he turned and gave the hand signal—motioning fingers like a person walking—which was rapidly passed back through the platoon. Suddenly a machine-gunner tripped a booby-trap wire: a grenade with the pin pulled and the firing lever held in place by the walls of an empty can it was shoved into. The wire, when snagged, pulled the primed grenade out, the firing lever flew off and the explosion was immediate. Fitted with an instantaneous fuse, the booby-trap was deadly simple and devastatingly effective. Harrison was four feet from the grenade when it exploded with a sharp, bright orange and red flash. The shock wave threw him several feet backwards and onto his right side. Fragments of metal sliced through his flesh like hot nails through butter. Four fragments punched through his chest, puncturing a lung. Smaller, matchhead-size pieces perforated his intestine and one penetrated the fleshy area beside his left eye.

Flashback: Ted Harrison—Scarcely able to breathe and panting like an exhausted dog, fighting to get air into lungs filling with blood. Someone's impaled me with a thick bamboo pole. Blood's seeping into my eye but I can still look downwards. What's that fluid oozing out of my chest? Can't breathe again, coughing and spitting up frothy blood. The pain's radiating outwards from my guts, flooding through my body. I curl up like a baby to try and stop the agony. Slide a hand down my pants—thank God, my balls are still there.

I can hear again but only in one ear. Voices yelling, 'Freeze, freeze—booby-traps!'

Someone's moaning … it's getting to me. Shut him up. Fucking shut him up, or I'll shoot the bastard.

There's a medic leaning over me. He's shaking and muttering and frantically trying to rip open a shell dressing. He's dropped it, poor bastard. He's dropped it again—twice in the dirt before he can wrap it around my chest and stomach.

Pain's subsiding a bit. There's a feeling of peace, I'm falling down a deep well. *Smack!* Someone's hit me across the face. The battalion doctor, Tony White, is sitting on me. He's shouting at me. 'Come on, get angry! Get angry, bugger you!' He hits me again.

The sharp end of the war caught Ted Harrison and almost punched the life out of him. In a bid to save him, the Assault Pioneers, on their way up the rock face to enemy bunkers on an adjacent slope, scrambled across to the C Company position and felled trees on a rocky ledge to get a dustoff aircraft in. Convulsing with pain, Harrison was given a tiny toothpaste-shaped morphine syrette by Tony White. An 'M' was scrawled on his forehead to tell hospital staff he'd been given the shot. Harrison's world went from near-death to wellbeing and clouds of cotton wool. His last recollection was of being slid into the bay of a chopper with a red cross on it and the medic pushing a lighted cigarette into his mouth. *That's a funny thing to offer a digger with a sucking chest wound …*

Alan 'Doggy' Dwyer was struggling to maintain his sense of humour. Two days spent walking through the weeds with a useless machine-gun had a sobering effect. Coming back through the wire at the Dat, each man cleared his weapon, but one veteran, a 'short-timer' with just days left in-country, noticed Dwyer had a sheepish look on his face instead of making his weapon safe.

'What the hell do ya mean, you can't cock it?' The soldier's eyes locked on the M60 and then, in disgust, on its carrier. 'You're supposed to test-fire every weapon before you come out here, fuckwit. Fire it into the pit in the Dat before you go out, dickhead—*got it?*'

The veteran looked at Dwyer, sizing up the best place to land a punch. 'I'm going home next week and now I find out I've been out looking for Charlie with a new guy who's got a '60 with no round up the spout. *Fuck me gently!*'

Dwyer noticed that men who had almost done their year's war got angry fast. He'd only spoken to a few since his arrival; they were a quiet, almost withdrawn lot. After the M60 episode, Dwyer made his mind up to get his act together and do things properly: for several hours he cleaned and oiled his Armalite—and made sure it cocked properly.

It was two days before the main body of his unit arrived. A soldier came running down through the company lines with a poncho wrapped around his body. It was part-way through the 25-minute afternoon downpour; the trench that acted as a drain between lines of tents was full of rushing brown water, and the rain on the tent tarpaulin was hammering so hard you couldn't speak. The soldier stuck his head in Dwyer's tent and shouted, 'You Dwyer, the new guy?'

Not a patrol again? Not an M60 again? Dwyer nodded.

'Get up to the Q store. You're going on TAOR patrol, and you're carrying the radio.'

Above: Arrival and departure at Luscombe Field. Troops were flown into the 1st Australian Task Force base at Nui Dat, often by Caribou aircraft shown in the picture. (Neil Moody)

Above: An Iroquois helicopter lifts troops out on an operation. Note the machine-gun and winch arm attached to the crowded aircraft. (Garry Davis)

Above: Aussie diggers take a rare opportunity to wash and shave in a jungle stream. (Garry Davis)

Right: Manna from Heaven...a resupply chopper delivers rations, replacement equipment and mail from home in a jungle clearing. (C Coy 3RAR Members)

Above: Alan 'Doggy' Dwyer, today a hero firefighter in Australia.
(Michael Perini of *The Sunday Telegraph*)
Inset: Alan Dwyer as a forward scout with 3RAR in Vietnam in 1971. (Alan Dwyer)

Above: Winching out the wounded using a jungle penetrator, a device on which the wounded soldier sat while being winched up to a hovering Dustoff helicopter. (SSG Victor Ward, FLATIRON Detachment, Fort Rucker, Alabama)

Below: More than a dozen troop-carrying Hueys line up at Luscombe Field to carry Australian infantry on operations. (The ANZAC Battalion)

Above: At 19, Colin Cogswell was wounded and awarded the Military Medal for bravery while serving with 5RAR in Vietnam during 1966–67. (Colin Cogswell)

Inset: Colin during a reflective moment at Nui Dat in 1966. (Colin Cogswell)

Above: Centurion tanks on jungle patrol in 1970. The tank was initially considered an unlikely asset in jungle warfare, but quickly proved its value with formidable firepower during contact with the enemy. (W. Matusch)

Above: The Australian soldier faced many rivers to cross during the jungle war. Members of 7 Platoon, C Coy 3RAR, prepare to ford the Song Rai River, one of the largest waterways in Phuoc Tuy Province. (Garry Davis)

Above: Wilf Matusch was attached to 2RAR/ANZAC Battalion when he was wounded in 1970. The young digger underwent and survived brain surgery as a result of shrapnel from an exploding booby trap. (W. Matusch)

Right: Wilf Matusch prepares for a tank patrol in Vietnam. (W. Matusch)

Left: Lieutenant David 'Patto' Paterson (far left) leader of 8 Platoon, C Coy 3RAR. Known as the 'Gentle Giant', the National Serviceman was one of the tallest Australian infantry platoon commanders to serve in South Vietnam. (Tony Cox)

Below: Rifleman and Assault Pioneer, Trevor Lynch, who was seriously wounded in action in the Nui Tai Vai Mountains in 1966 while serving with 5RAR. (K. Chester)

JIMMY'S BIG FALL

Good memories fade fast. Bad ones stay in the mind, even intensify. Inside your head can be a dangerous place; paranoia grows like mould, particularly when you return to scenes of traumatic events—like the Australian soldier doing a second tour. And more so, like the combatant going out in the weeds for a second time. Those who did a second tour are still looked at today like they have two heads; misfits, crazy. *What the bloody hell would induce a man to go back for another year in the Funny Farm?* Many a veteran would send his father, his mother, his uncle, even his wife or girl-friend to Vietnam before he'd go back.

'Tour of Duty': another piece of Namstalgia, a military way of expressing commitment, doing good things in the service of Australia. A 'tour' conjures up bus rides through the country, pub meals, a good look around at the sights and the locals. No Vietnam veteran ever considered he'd been on a 'tour'.

Jimmy Griffiths was doing his second tour. He'd been in Vietnam in 1967 with the First Australian Task Force HQ. He was back in 1971 with 3rd Battalion. No real problem for Jimmy, a career soldier who joined the Army in the early 1960s because his grandmother told him to 'do something useful'. She also bet him £10 he wouldn't do it. He got five quid, and years after Grandmother's death was still waiting for the other five.

Griffiths, born in Kilmarnock—the home of Johnnie Walker whisky—came to Australia aged 14 and settled in Perth. He farm-laboured until he accepted Grandma's bet and signed on for six years.

Griffiths was not built like a pugilist, but he could fight like a thrashing machine and had been a 'Golden Gloves' boxing champion. This was one ability that slightly hampered his promotion in the Army: he was renowned for 'snotting' people, particularly those who pissed him off, and they were usually senior in rank.

'I remember him,' Griffiths would say. 'I snotted him.' He went up and down the promotional ladder from Lance-Corporal to Sergeant so often, he kept separate sets of uniforms with the different stripes sewn on them.

In Vietnam, 1971, he became Sergeant Griffiths, but he soon came close to snotting an officer, and was posted to Administration Company as the helicopter padmaster. He loaded or back-loaded the Hueys that continuously came into the Nui Dat chopper pad. Here the talents and true nature of Jimmy Griffiths shone. The man was a born hustler—with a heart of gold. As padmaster, he was able to 'borrow' hard-to-obtain items. This was a military skill some men aspired to; others were naturals and could obtain anything through an underground bartering system that flourished in the military. Jimmy had honed his skills during his time with 3rd Battalion in Malaya.

In Vietnam, borrowing—and plain thieving—to help your mates was elevated to an art form. At the extreme end of the spectrum was the black market: soap, Salem cigarettes, radios, fans and stereos from the PX stores, all purchased or pinched and sold on the streets of Saigon and Vung Tau at inflated prices. The penalty for black marketeering was severe. Griffiths did not dabble in that, but he would ensure by fair means or foul that all the necessary equipment and some luxuries went out to those men enduring tough times in the jungle. Some said Jimmy Griffiths was the best bloke God ever shovelled guts into, and there was a reason—other than his acquisitions ability—for this.

Embarkation point for air supply to the men in the field was from the chopper pad that Griffiths had christened 'Teeny Weeny Airlines'. Down here, next to the landing area, Griffiths had placed a bunch of empty cartons. Each week or so the boxes would magically fill up with combat rations, dropped there by soldiers going on operations. The boxes contained cans of food the diggers didn't want to be weighed down even further with: ham and lima beans, date rolls, and meatballs in tomato sauce— puke food. These rations found their way, via Griffiths' Land-Rover, to a former French monastery in Dat Do, a medium-sized town a few clicks south-east of Nui Dat. Here, Griffiths and a few mates were quietly caring for those who had been dealt one of life's losing hands. The monastery was an orphanage; a place for lost or abandoned babies and toddlers—those condemned to be the most innocent victims of the Vietnam War. A handful of Catholic nuns and a Vietnamese priest cared for the children, some of whom were light-skinned, with distinctive Eurasian and Afroasian features—the offspring of hasty sexual encounters between Western soldiers and local bargirls. The kids were always hungry. Griffiths put the word out among the soldiers. 'Any spare tucker, drop it in the boxes and I'll zip it over to the kids next time I'm off to the Horseshoe.'

Griffiths was a small man, so small you'd miss him in the bush but for an extraordinary physical feature: he had the biggest ears in the battalion. They were like open car doors—'Bilby', some men called him after the huge-eared marsupial. The protruberances complemented his grin, and if there is such a thing as a Scottish smile, the padmaster had it. He'd grin at the orphans and let them hang off his ears. Sometimes he put the kids down in the dirt in front of him and, to shrieks of delight, wiggled those ears.

In the first few months of his tour of duty, Griffiths built up a rapport with the priest. The side benefit, he quickly discovered, was that the man of God also had a unique gift for supplying Benedictine liqueur. The small bunch of Good Samaritans acquired blankets and sheets, pillows and toiletries for the Dat Do children, and began to feel they were contributing by making life a bit easier for the less fortunate—until the day at the monastery when the priest came running. 'Jimmy, VC coming, go now!'

Griffiths gunned the Land-Rover along the Dat Do road and heard the bullets zing overhead. He made it back to the ATF, but the Vietcong made an example of the priest: they shot him in the head.

Flashback: Jimmy Griffiths—Walking back through the lines of tents. This joint stinks. Been here, done it all before. *Made a big mistake coming back.* Just look at the tents, every one bloody rotten. There's the one I slept in two friggin' years ago. Phuoc Tuy gets worse every year we stay here. Bombed, burnt, polluted. The hills we saw on the first tour were covered with lush greenness. Now you can see the rock face, defoliated, shot to hell. Every landmark is filled with grief. The Warbies out west—there's an operation going on up there now. How many dead so far? Hundreds of the poor bastards have already been cut up since we started this war. The big question: am I going to become a casualty stat this time? *Didn't get you last time Uc Da Loi, get you this time …* Another place of interest we 'discovered' on the last guided tour: the Long Green, down south near the coast. Sand, low scrub, a thousand tracks and trails—every one seeded with landmines. Remember the Horseshoe, the old volcanic caldera turned into an Australian firebase, bunkers for us grunts deep in the lava walls, artillery in the middle? And the Mine Fence, the multi-belted barbed-wire entanglement laced liberally with M16 jumping-jack mines that ran all the way to the South China Sea. 'Got to keep the Nogs away from the villagers.' Probably kept the bludgers in, truth be told. It was the sickest joke of the war as far as the Aussies were concerned—the Nogs stole the mines by the thousand and blew us up with our own bloody ordnance. Then there's the fire trails up north, stretches of J sprayed with defoliant to stop Charlie hiding. Miles of fire trails, including the mighty Firestone Trail, a mud freeway heavy with Agent Orange. If the snipers and enemy mines didn't get you on the Firestone, the poison the planes dropped would get you in the long run.

Many men died in Vietnam, they just didn't know it until years after they got home.

But maybe we can still have a good time—stir up the locals and get stoked in Vungas. Remember the Blue Lagoon, the New York Bar, chomping steak and chips at the Beachcomber Club? Put shit on the Yank MPs but keep the heck out of their way. The Aussie MPs were good: they'd just give you a kick in the arse and drop you back at the R and C Centre. Pull the flap back, look in the tent—there's a smell of fungus. Mould sooner or later infects everything, including your skin. And there's another smell: the pissaphone pipes and the latrines. That's Vietnam—one big stink. Welcome back, Jimmy.

Griffiths had every reason to regret his return. He was enduring the wildest ride of his life in a Huey heading at full throttle towards the province of Long Khan. The padmaster told himself repeatedly that he shouldn't be here, hanging onto his arse in this shuddering machine.

June 7, Long Khan, and B Company, 3RAR was fighting for its life part-way through one of the biggest enemy bunkers the Australians had ever walked into. It was so big, Centurion tanks were sent in. Worse, the occupants—hardcore NVA—were hanging in, and a firefight had been going on for hours under the huge tree canopy. The bunker system was 1000 metres square. Fifty troops from the 3/33 NVA Regiment had dug in and, pouring every bit of firepower they had onto the tanks, were still in close-quarter combat with Bravo Company. Three of the tank crew were wounded; five Rifle Company men were also down. The rifle company's forward observer—the man responsible for directing artillery fire—was dead. The Australians had nearly exhausted their ammunition, down to their last 20-round maga-zine. The call went back to the Dat: *get here fast with more ammo or B Company will pay dearly …*

Padmaster Griffiths jumped aboard the resupply Huey with boxes of ammunition. He couldn't wait for whoever it was that normally flew out with the resupply chopper. Ahead, circling like sharks, Griffiths saw three Bushranger gunships pouring fire into the bunkers to allow the desperate diggers an opportunity to pull back. One Bushranger dropped out, the resupply Iroquois took its place in the loop, and Griffiths clung on as the Australian pilot banked and went in for the drop.

The two other men in the chopper had also seen their share of service. The door gunner, hanging over the twin M60s, was David Dubber, a corporal on his second tour of Vietnam, just like Griffiths. During his first tour he'd been Mentioned in Dispatches for courage. The pilot, Flight Captain Lance, had flown with the South African Air Force, where he'd been awarded a Distinguished Flying Cross and Air Medal during the Korean War. He had been recruited to the RAAF because of a chronic shortage of pilots.

Lance slowed his machine to a hover and the padmaster went into action. He knew the routine: while the chopper was still, dump as close as possible to where the friendlies are—usually marked by a coloured smoke grenade.

Griffiths suddenly felt a 'bee sting' in his thigh. The aircraft erupted, with pieces of aluminum and fibreglass flying upwards as the floor was torn to pieces. The last thing Griffiths saw was Lance jerk and slump over his controls before the Huey turned on its side. Jimmy plunged out of the passenger bay, twisted and rolled 35 metres through the air, hit the tallest trees, and bounced and tumbled before slamming into the earth—6 metres from an enemy bunker. His spine was fractured in two places, 37 other bones were smashed, and his ribs punctured his lungs. The Iroquois plunged through the trees and burst into flames, killing Lance and Dubber.

Flashback: Jimmy Griffiths—Gasping, gasping for air. Hell, if I'd landed on a Vietcong I would probably get a bloody medal. The face above me is Bravo Company's platoon sergeant, Garry Mathieson's. He's pushing a cigarette into my mouth. That's funny, he's a fitness fanatic, he doesn't smoke ... Struggling to regain clear thought but engulfed by the pain. I start screaming. A morphine syrette is pushed into my arm and the world's going fuzzy. I can hear the rattle of gunfire, see the wreck of the chopper. There's another chopper above, a dustoff, whipping the trees. Some sort of canvas wrap-around is under and around me. The winch is pulling me up to the dustoff. I can see the door gunner watching, guiding me through the trees as I go up, up ...

THE CHICKEN MAN

'Dustoff', 'casevac', 'medivac'—Vietnam acronyms, buzzwords that meant one thing: if you go down in the weeds, we'll get you out. And it was true, for in no war before Vietnam could you so quickly get from the field to the operating table, to be treated by the top surgeons in the world. Fifteen minutes, 30 tops—the Australian or American dustoff was in, and you were out. Minus half your stomach, a leg, an arm, or flattened by heat stroke, the Iroquois was there, in a clearing or at the hover over the tall timber, with a jungle penetrator that punched its way through the treetops. After it touched the ground and discharged its static electricity, it was safe to fold down the seat-like contraption, sit the wounded man on it and let the crewman winch him up. There was also the Stokes Litter, a steel basket as long as a coffin, and a canvas sling that fully enclosed the soldier like a cocoon. Morphine drip in, you were hitting 100 knots or more on your way to 'Vampire'—the 36th Evacuation Hospital in Vung Tau.

The Royal Australian Army Medical Corps had established a cluster of medical elements near the sea at Vung Tau. It was initially crewed by 2 Field Ambulance, then 8 Field, until finally it became the 1st Australian Field Hospital. Each of these medical units was given the radio call-sign 'Vampire'. The first Australian Field Hospital consisted of 106 beds: a medical and a surgical ward each accommodated 50 patients, and an Intensive Care Unit housed six. There were two theatres, Triage and Operating, as well as X-ray, Psychiatry, Pathology, Pharmacy, Physiotherapy, Dental and Hygiene units.

Little was known about the 'bloody angels', the men and women who worked at the blood and guts end of the war. No grunt ever wanted to see the inside of either Vampire or 36 Evac—but often said a silent prayer to thank God for them being there. Even the dimmest digger had some idea of what the

medical teams had to deal with after a firefight or a mine incident. Battle casualties in Phuoc Tuy could be ten or twenty at a
time. And these medical teams were dealing with some different
battle injuries to those of previous wars, such as 'high-velocity
missile device' wounds. Some surgical techniques were at the cutting edge of war trauma, light years ahead of World War II. This
was necessary to improve the mortality ratio, as the latest weapons
of war—a bullet travelling at 3000 feet per second; white-hot
shrapnel from a mortar or artillery shell—were designed to rip a
soldier apart. In Vietnam the enemy had worked out that it
wasn't necessary to always kill the Australian or American
soldier—they only had to wound him badly enough to get him
out of the action, and tie up valuable resources in doing so. Hence
the proliferation of mines and booby-traps that maimed: the
shrapnel of nuts and bolts that took a toe, a foot, a finger or the
eyes. Charlie was brilliant at fighting dirty, and this presented a
whole new set of challenges for the medical teams at Vung Tau.

The hospitals were sacred ground, inhabited by angels. From
1966 to the middle of 1967, only six of the 220 battle casualties
died after admission—but with the wounds they had suffered,
they were never going to make it anyway.

Ted Harrison was what medical staff described as 'seriously ill'.
The dustoff flight from the rock ledge on Nui Thi Vai to the
chopper pad at 36th Evac had been a blur to him, lying on the
stretcher in the Huey's wind-blasted passenger bay. But he could
now feel the chill of the stainless-steel table, hear the urgent whispering of the medical team and the sound of scissors slicing
through his filthy, stinking uniform. The medic swabbed him
down with a huge cotton ball soaked in a yellowy antiseptic.
Then came a Catholic priest, whispering about absolution.

Jesus, I'm dead already.

The last memory Edmund Harrison had that day was of the needle going in, and the certainty he was to be no more.

For hours the surgical team worked on him, removing four large grenade fragments from his left lung. One rib was removed and a further four were broken to get at the shrapnel. Two fragments were left in Harrison's body, considered too deep to get at. After further work on the perforations in his small intestine, he was closed up with surgical wire and wheeled into recovery.

Not far from Ted's bed was Trevor Lynch, also 'seriously ill'. Lynch looked like a snowman: the front of his body, a mass of lacerations, was swathed in bandages and his head was almost completely covered. There was no sound.

A few days later, two Army officers arrived at a house in Blacktown, western Sydney, with a telegram.

MELBOURNE TLX VIC 12-42P...ACKNOWLEDGE DELI-VERY...MRS A R HARRISON...WOUNDED IN ACTION AND PLACED ON SERIOUSLY ILL LIST BUT NOT VERY SERIOUSLY ILL LIST...STOP

IT IS LEARNED WITH REGRET THAT YOUR SON 215812 LANCE COPORAL EDMUND WILLIAM DENNIS HARRISON WAS PLACED ON THE SERIOUSLY ILL LIST AT 36 EVACUATION HOSPITAL VUNG TAU VIETNAM ON 17 OCTOBER 1966 AS A RESULT OF FRAGMENTATION WOUNDS RECEIVED IN ACTION IN PHUOC TUY PROVINCE VIETNAM...STOP

FURTHER PROGRESS REPORTS WILL BE SENT TO YOU AT REGULAR INTERVALS BUT SHOULD A CHANGE OF CONDITION OCCUR YOU WILL BE NOTIFIED IMME-DIATELY...ARMY HEADQUARTERS (15 215812 36 17TH 1966) 1255.

★★★★★★★★★★★★★★★★★★★★★★★★★★

Doggy Dwyer felt that at last he'd got a handle on this war. He'd just got off to a bad start, what with the M60 stuffing up—hell, that wasn't his fault anyway—and the radio signaller's job for a day, which was no problem. Now he was back to his original job: forward scout, the most dangerous job in Infantry. He was determined to make a go of it.

He scanned the bush ahead. His arc of responsibility, his world as a scout, was 180 degrees. Immediate front: trip wires, punji pits with sharp, urine-soaked stakes. Middle ground and shoulder height: an enemy suddenly standing. Middle distance: moving shadows in the trees ahead. Dwyer moved silently, panning his Armalite left to right, his eyes moving with the rifle. Mouth and ears wide open to catch the sounds of the bush—foot down, stop, listen, foot up, pan left and right again, eyes always following the barrel. The scout also has to think ahead, always have a pre-planned move; check out fire positions he could dive for in the event of contact. Stop now and turn, look back to the section commander, who's checking his compass and map. *Fuck, he's not looking at me, he's shagging about with his bloody compass. I need an eye up my arse to do this job. Look at me!* Dwyer was given a wave of the hand for direction and a wave left to get back on compass bearing. *Ah, at last he's waving me. Forward 50, go left 20 ... this is like doing the military two-step. Now pick out an extra-big tree and move to that, scanning the arc.*

Ahead was a fallen log. From it came the sound of scraping. The scout could just see a head of black hair moving—*Vietcong digging behind the log. Rifle up, finger on the trigger. One shot, one kill.* Suddenly the black hair shot up and a bush turkey jumped onto the log, followed a moment later by its mate. The birds were as startled as Dwyer.

Dwyer knew all about birds, especially chickens—he was a de-beaker by trade.

His father, Clyde, had been in the Kokoda campaign in World War II, and suffered what was called 'war neurosis'.

'The Army's good,' he told Alan, 'but only in peacetime.'

Without doubt, Clyde was suffering severe post-traumatic stress, and things only got worse when the builder who was to construct the family home at Mortdale went belly-up, taking Clyde's savings with him. The family had to live in a tent on a vacant block.

Later, the Dwyers moved to Badgery's Creek and started a small poultry holding. Clyde died at the age of 58. 'He simply ran out of life,' Alan told friends. Mother, Yvonne, sold eggs door to door while her son sought work at a nearby poultry farm. Here he developed his sense of humour, catching and de-beaking chickens. He would take the five-week-old chick and trim its beak, then push its face onto a hot-plate and cauterise what was left of the beak. He was Badgery's Creek's top chicken de-beaker, so good that other poultry farms called for him at de-beaking time. It was a sit-at-the-workbench job; the monotony was broken by cleaning out the manure trays on the coops and jumping up and down on your haunches catching armfuls of flapping birds to put in cardboard boxes for market.

Then one day Dwyer decided it was time to move on—he needed a life. When asked why he didn't sign on to the Army for the full six years, the gun chicken de-beaker replied, 'I'll see if I like it first.'

Flashback: Doggy Dwyer—May 14: Sitting here in the jungle, dog-tired after another bad night. Men are spooning beans out of cans, heating a brew over a pebble of C4 explosive—a bit dangerous, but very effective, and a bloody sight better than that Hexamine shit.

I just remembered something nobody else remembered. Where is it? I know it's here somewhere. Here—pound cake in a tin.

Open it carefully and push a waterproof match into the top of the spongy cake. Look around, no-one watching, light the match with the Zippo and watch it flare and burn brightly—'Happy birthday to me, happy twentieth birthday to me ...'

UNDER FIRE

Those here before had left in a hurry, like they had picked up their bags and just walked out without looking back at the tents they had lived in, on and off, for a year. What was left was the background debris: a broom, a few rusted coat-hangers, an empty ration-can ashtray and four mosquito nets—worn so thin they almost crumbled to the touch—strung over sagging cots. Outside, nailed to a tree, was a washstand, now leaning at a crazy angle; the last soldier couldn't be bothered to fix it. That was the good thing about when your time was up—some other bloke could make and mend.

The rows of four-man tents had sat here under the rubber trees like a line of filthy arrival and departure lounges for five years; yawning vacant now, waiting for the next travellers. At the end of 12 months, a bunch of buggered, war-traumatised men would depart the lines and a new group would arrive, debussing from trucks on the red-earthed road. Nui Dat Task Force base was like a clearing house full of nomads. Most of the men in these tents would spend only a fraction of the year sleeping on the World War II-style stretchers—steel beds came later—because Vietnam was a very active 12-month war that demanded the grunt be out in the jungle on operations.

If these tents could speak … They were erected in 1966 by 5th and 6th battalions, and were still here when 3rd and 4th battalions fought the war's endgame in 1971.

Flashback: Wilf Matusch—Sitting on a campstool at a table writing a letter home, tent illuminated by two naked bulbs powered by a generator somewhere. Sucking on a Salem, smoke drifting out the sides of the tent. An estate agent would describe this place 'set among a boulevard of trees, a room with a view and fully aerated'. This is home—a tent sheet thrown over a set of poles surrounded by a double layer of sandbags. At one end of the tent there's an entrance, sandbagged in dog-leg fashion to prevent shrapnel from an exploding shell flying in and killing the men inside. There's three other diggers in the tent with me, but not tonight. They're all up the boozer guzzling VB and XXXX. A portable transistor radio is tuned in to Armed Forces Radio playing requests—'Mountain Of Love' by Johnny Rivers and 'I Hear A Symphony' by The Supremes. Vietnam's all about music. When the others come back, half smashed, they'll fire up the Real Music—Creedence and The Stones. What a blast, through these state-of-the-art, reel-to-reel Akai 10 tape decks, Pioneer turntables and Sansui amps with a wattage output that makes the sandbags shake. The stereo, brought back from R and R in Singapore and Hong Kong, was sandbagged into the walls of the tent along with sets of speakers, woofing and tweeting. Sometimes, by midnight, the whole battalion's letting it rip. No-one in the upper echelons seems to complain. Maybe they figure the VC, eating his rice a click outside the wire, is scratching his head and ready to *didi mau*.

Next morning, Matusch dropped his letter in with the battalion postie, hoisted his pack and headed down to the chopper pad. The last thing he did before closing the tent flap was to throw a blanket over the Akai.

The Vietnam 'Cook's Tour' brochure described the topography of Phuoc Tuy:
    … generally flat, with a gradual increase in vegetation north from the coastal regions. There are elevated, rocky landmasses in the south, south-west and extreme north-east—referred to as the Long Hais, Nui Thi Vais and Nui May Taos. As well as the higher features, there are a few knolls, each generally named Nui Dat (small hill). Low mangrove swamps are located in the south-west, at Rung Sat. Most agricultural land is in the southern section of

Phuoc Tuy, with heavy vegetation covering the hills that rise to the north. A quarter of the province is under cultivation … much of the jungle area is secondary growth, laced with bamboo—which covers three-quarters of the province.

Whoever compiled the information obviously did so from the seat of a high-flying aircraft, and had no concept of what was unravelling below in an area that measured about 60 kilometres by 40 kilometres—and the fact that men were going to hump across every back-breaking metre of it.

The geographer also missed something else: as a war zone, it was unique. The fighting here in the 1960s was sporadic, like a plague of bushfires. As the years passed, these grew into larger, fiercer blazes consuming ever-greater resources, but the war remained a series of fragmented battles. 'We're chasing and killing Gooks from the Delta to the DMZ,' one American commander said, referring to the southern-most district of South Vietnam, the Mekong Delta, and to the northern extermity of the war, the Demilitarised Zone. And, to the frustration of the Allied Forces, that's the way it remained—a series of conflagrations that couldn't be stamped out, from section-sized firefights to major battalion-strength engagements.

It was all happening, as you saw from the air, under jungle canopy, in open fields and up in the mountains. South Vietnam was on fire.

Wilf Matusch was solidly-built, topped six feet and sported a David Niven-style pencil moustache. He was also one of the Army's most skilful visual trackers. By the time he reached Vietnam, he could follow a trail left by a man—moving across almost any terrain—at 1000 metres an hour. That was considered by the Army Tracking Wing instructors at the Infantry Training Centre in Sydney to be 'patrol pace'. Matusch later became an instructor himself, teaching Infantrymen how to pick up a sign on the ground and follow it. With constant practice you could equal the skill of an Australian Aboriginal tracker.

Matusch excelled in stalking a fleeing 'enemy' in Australia, but in Vietnam things didn't follow a script. Now jammed between two massive bamboo stalks that held him like a vice, he had neither the energy nor the inclination to take part in this war any longer. He was the most buggered he'd ever felt in his life, and this was the thickest, ugliest country he had ever seen. In Australia he'd heard about jungle; he'd seen it in *Tarzan* movies, looked at pictures in books—thick, green, dripping moisture, pristine. The slopes of Nui Dinh Mountain—part of the Warburtons—were a mass of wait-a-while vines, topped by double-canopy jungle, beneath which were clumps of bamboo that had been growing since Stone Age man stomped through here—but Stone Age man had more sense than to come near this place. Matusch hung between the bamboo stalks until his coverman John Bolste, freed him. Matusch whispered, 'Thanks'. Bolste covered the tracker while he searched for visual signs. Once Matusch found something—a leaf turned over, a boot-print, broken saplings, ants defending a broken nest—he would call forward the tracking dog with his handler. Man and dog would pursue the enemy at speed while the rifle platoon followed up, ready for a firefight.

A few hours later, the enemy rewrote the script again: ahead was a ravine—and a few minutes away loomed a monsoonal storm. *What the hell else can go wrong?* Matusch thought, peering across the ravine where the enemy was obviously waiting for the dopey Australians to follow.

Murphy's Law ran the Vietnam War. If something was going to go wrong in the war zone, it went wrong in huge lumps, and the foot soldier always copped it worst. Overlooking a ravine on Nui

Dinh, facing off the Vietcong, a platoon of exhausted diggers were about to get soaked.

One more problem: nothing to eat. Matusch and the combat tracking team had full rations—36 individual meals between the four-man team. Problem was, the rifle platoon of 25 men had nothing. They had missed their chopper resupply by opting instead to follow up a group of VC who had probed their platoon position the night before. So the trackers busted open their packs and shared their food. Tea, coffee and sugar were pooled, cans of meat were opened and passed around, and rice was quickly cooked. Everyone was able to get some hot food in before the heavens opened up on them.

Matusch settled down in the blackness to try and sleep, despite being drenched. He inserted the ear piece of his transistor radio and switched onto the AFVN Radio. It was time for 'The Adventures of Chicken Man'. He decided that even a partial doze was out of the question, so instead chose to catch up on the radio cartoon character before starting a two-hour sentry on the machine-gun. Doubtless the VC were still across the gully, sleeping with one eye open and trained on the Australian position.

Next morning, fog on the mountain and no resupply ration drop, again. As the day wore on, the hunger pangs grew. That afternoon, the chopper came in and searched for a hole in the jungle canopy. Ten days straight on rations, and regulations stated the troops in the J had to have fresh food. Down from the choppers—along with C ration packs—came one stale salad roll and an orange for each man. The Army had fulfilled its fresh food obligations.

The second son of German migrants, Cornelia and Wilfred Matusch, young Wilf arrived in Australia on his third birthday. His parents spent the first Australian money they exchanged on a block of Cadbury chocolate for their son. It cost threepence,

Cornelia reminded Wilf every birthday thereafter. There was a military history in the Matusch family—not one you advertised in Australia in 1953, but a proud background nevertheless. Father had fought with the German Army on the Russian front in World War II, and Grandfather Matusch had been a fighter pilot in the German Air Force in World War I. But Wilfred and Cornelia, weary of war and displacement, decided to leave Europe and seek a better, more settled life for their children in Australia.

It didn't remain settled, though: the couple divorced in 1960, and Cornelia remarried Emmanuel Wheatley. The family then settled in Port Kembla, on the NSW south coast. Home was at the foot of a hill on Red Point, known to the locals as 'Hill 60'. Red Point had been part of the Australian coastal fortification system during World War II: it was dotted with abandoned concrete bunkers, pillboxes and, even more intriguing for a bunch of kids, interconnecting tunnels that ran between gun emplacements. In this 'war zone', you could wipe out the opposition with toy pistols and, later, air rifles firing real BB slugs. Below the old fortifications were surf beaches and some of the best spear-fishing on the coast. Life in Port Kembla may have been a struggle for working-class families, but it was heaven for the kids. It was here that Matusch dreamed of a military career.

Flashback: Wilf Matusch—Anzac Day Service at school assembly, Port Kembla. I'm eight years old and sit enraptured as the headmaster recalls the Anzac legend. It was courage, valour, mateship, men crawling forward in the face of murderous fire. It was ANZAC Cove, Gallipoli, April 25, 1915, birth of a nation. Peter, my brother, nudges me in the ribs—'Wilf, you and me are the bad guys in this story. Father and Grandfather are the enemies they're talking about.'

At age 17 Wilf Matusch took the plunge and decided to join the Australian Regular Army—become a professional soldier, follow family tradition, maybe accept a commission. Be a bit like Vic Morrow in the TV series 'Combat'. Matusch got into the Army, but it was nothing like Sergeant Saunders in 'Combat', and the war he expected to be part of bore no resemblance to the World Wars that Father and Grandfather had fought in.

Three days after his twentieth birthday, he sat wide-eyed and vertical in a Huey with a combat tracking team, speeding across the jungle tree tops at 100 knots. A New Zealand rifle platoon doing its tour as part of 2 Battalion had hit a bunker system. Two Kiwis were already dead and the VC had dug in, throwing everything at the New Zealanders. After hours of bunker-to-bunker fighting in the jungle, Bushranger gunships had been called in and the battle had developed into a full-blown firefight. The call went out for trackers.

Flashback: Wilf Matusch—0800 hours and the Huey comes clattering in towards a small clearing, where red smoke marks the LZ. It's a hot insertion and no sooner has the chopper bounced on landing and put us on the ground than the machine is in fuck-off-quick mode. I listen for the distinct crack and thump—crack gives you direction. The pause between crack and thump gives the range. *Crack crack.* Rounds pass over, sounding like a stock whip across the top of the head. Johnno and I make for the trees. We both slump. I call to him, 'They shooting at us?'

'I think so.'

More rounds fly.

'If I get it today, will you write and tell Lyn what happened?'

Johnno: 'Yeah, okay. And if I get chopped will you write and tell my mum?'

'Yeah, okay. Let's go!'

The New Zealanders of 2 Platoon, Victor Company had been in the fight of their lives. And it was still on, with Bushranger gunships sweeping in low, and that unmistakable long ripping sound of mini-guns pouring lead into the enemy; it sounded like a long fart. The choppers, having expended all their ammunition, turned like angry hornets for the flight home. Matusch and 'Johnno' Johnson worked their way with the other trackers into the jungle, where the foliage had been shredded by high-velocity bullets. Smoke hung in the air and burnt the nostrils; trees were bent, buckled and ripped apart by gunship fire.

The Kiwi section commander, Corporal Roly Horopappera, a don't-mess-about Maori with a build to match, pushed the two Aussies down. 'You blokes smoke, yeah? Have a smoke, we got a few of these skinny little bastards to get out the bunkers yet. Then we got a few scores to settle ... they killed two of my men.'

Earlier, Horopappera had been faced with an Infantry commander's most difficult tactical situation: calling in air support while engaged in a firefight on the ground. The pilots of the gunships and Phantom jets, loaded with high explosive or napalm, had to drop their load through thick canopy on an unseen enemy—without blasting their own troops. Air support accuracy relied solely on smoke grenades thrown by friendlies at ground level, so that aircraft could aim in front, or across the front, of the coloured smoke.

Immediately upon striking the bunkers, Horopappera's section—no less than nine men—had sighted the VC, but not the 105mm unexploded shell at shoulder height strung in the trees. The VC used a bamboo trigger with torch batteries to command-detonate the bomb. The explosion killed the two lead men. A wall of enemy fire then pinned down the remainder of the section. Hugging the ground, the section commander repeatedly crawled forward to try and pull back his dead and wounded. 'He disappeared in a hail of fire, rolled and rolled again, went forward, got a bloke and came back,' said one of the survivors, who added as an afterthought: '"Roly" … it's a good name, eh, bro?'

Horopappera then threw smoke and called in the Bushrangers, which strafed across his front. The big Kiwi called for more fire, this time at 'danger close' range. The pilot refused, insisting Horopappera pull back. So the section commander simply passed the smoke grenades back among his men and the 'tail-end Charlie'—the last man—popped them to his rear. 'Okay, we're back now,' the New Zealander grunted into his radio. 'Come in!'

Believing the section had withdrawn, the pilot unleashed a stream of mini-gun fire that tore ten metres in front of the NZ soldiers.

'Yeah, it was real close, but we couldn't even blink with the Nog fire. We were absolutely fucked anyway,' Roly said later.

The search began for the Vietcongs' escape route. Matusch swept the ground, identifying bootprints—*New Zealand tread, no good. I'm not working in a sterile zone. Need a clear area.* The visual tracker worked his way outwards in a 'private search' with a Victor Company soldier covering him. The Aussie moved with a crouched, hunched-over posture, scanning the ground and surrounding bush. He suddenly pulled up. Just ahead, lying on a sandy track, was a human brain. The Kiwi coverman came closer to Matusch with a sorry look on his face and whispered almost apologetically, 'That's our lead scout's brain … his face was blown away by the 105 shell, mate. It fell out when we were getting him in the chopper.'

Matusch stood dumbstruck as the next Australian tracker wandered up quietly. 'How's it goin'?' he asked under his breath, and went to move on.

The Kiwi stopped him with his rifle. 'Would you mind not standing on my mate's brain ...'

The Australian stepped back like he'd just shoved his foot in boiling water. He gaped at the sight, chin on his chest.

Matusch tried to shake the image from his mind. He moved off into the jungle, stopped and knelt, examining what was before him. A picture emerged like a photo coming into focus in a developing tray: the visual tracker cast his eyes up and then left and right, looking for signs of a logical way for men to make off quickly. First, top sign: looking for leaves and bushes at waist and shoulder height pushed in the wrong direction, like cat fur brushed the wrong way. Nothing too obvious. Next, ground sign. Yes! A bootprint, then another, with just the heel showing; then a toe print where the front foot of the Vietcong dug in at high speed. *Measure the distance of the pace. Yes, definitely moving quickly. Now a small bush bent sideways. A plant crushed underfoot. Check the bootprints again. Three, four, five, could be six enemy.*

Matusch stood and moved forward a couple more paces, with the Kiwi rifleman following silently behind. *Slight breeze left to right, that means the enemy's scent will have shifted two or three metres, and when the dog picks up the smell it won't be on the visual sign. Remember that.*

Suddenly, confirmation: two spots of bright blood. Matusch turned and clicked his fingers. 'Johnno, bring the dog up, we're onto them!'

WAR GAMES

Doggy Dwyer was looking at the limp, twisted body on the ground—the first man he'd seen killed in battle. His platoon moved up to C Company, who had just been in a fierce contact with the Vietcong. Six VC were dead, spread around a fork in the track, bundles of black clothing and automatic weapons, many shattered by the Australians' fire, lay on the track and in the bush. This was the sharp end of the war, but it felt nothing like a battle zone. It wasn't like the movies, there was no control over territory—just get it all together and move on to the next objective.

For a moment, what really interested Dwyer was the reactions of the men who carried out, or witnessed, the killing. Shooting the enemy was very matter-of-fact on paper. On the sneaker range at Canungra, it was like popping ducks at a fairground shooting gallery. On a sandy track in Phuoc Tuy, though, there was an unreality about such random death.

This is what we are here to do. This is what we do here.

Nothing in training prepares a 19-year-old for his first meeting with death. There was no trauma training, no visit to the local morgue to see what a real corpse looks like. No-one ever said, 'A body will look like this—this is what happens when people die.'

Soldiers look at other dead soldiers, but they don't really want to look. It's more like a sidle-up while puffing madly on a cigarette, take a glance, then scurry away and check your equipment, or make a quick brew and chain-smoke another five cigarettes. Get busy, do something—but no discussion at all about the dead lying metres away.

Remember back in Australia during one of the bore-us-stupid character lectures, the ones they gave after they found that in the Korean War men wilted after combat from what they'd done; what they'd seen too much of?

The paramount thought that goes through a soldier's mind when he looks at the dead or seriously wounded—be it friend or enemy—is, *thank God it wasn't me.* The second thought: *we killed the enemy.* Never *I killed an enemy.* A firefight was always a shared experience.

Dwyer had to look. The VC soldier was about 20 years old. The colour had already drained from his body; the skin looked like dirty canvas. He lay naked from the waist up. There were no visible bullet holes—a soldier had laid a banana leaf over the exit wounds in his back. Soldiers had already turned over the body using toggle ropes; many a dying Vietcong would pull the pin from a grenade and placed it under his body, to hold the firing lever closed. Get too close, roll the corpse over and the grenade explodes—the enemy's last act of defiance.

Dwyer saw that death in war was undignified—and frighteningly sudden. The C Company Scout had been the first to open fire on the VC group—and he'd found time to place his shots well.

Men moved away from the killing ground. They knew what would come next, and tried to look busy to avoid it: scrape out shallow graves and lay the dead men down.

Army padres rewrote the Fifth Commandment: 'Thou shalt not kill' became 'Thou shalt not commit murder'.

That's made us all feel better; the fact that the Army has God on its side. And the old Army cliché of 'train hard, fight easy' took on a new meaning here on the sandy track: what the Army needed in training was a spot of carnage and trauma preparation.

The other thing about battle death is the black humour.

Flashback: Doggy Dwyer—Two men charged with digging a hole are hacking and shovelling dirt with the Army entrenching tool—a small, fold-up shovel.

'Bugger it, I had this job after the last shitfight, an' he gives it me again,' one says, nodding toward his platoon sergeant. 'And last time it was digging up a dead Nog to look for documents. Chrissake, I wrapped a shell dressing around my face to kill the stink and still wanted to vomit for a friggin' week. Why me again?'

The other soldier: 'Because you're getting good at it ... and because the Sarge just likes givin' you the shits. 'The pair dig on, then: 'I can see the next letter I write home—Mum, Dad, buried another Nog today, only three million to go ...'

They drag the body into the hole.

'You know you can't bury him face down?'

'Why the bloody hell not? He's cactus, why would he give a stuff?'

'It's offensive to the Nogs' religion, dickhead. Jeepers, mate, you don't know nothing do ya ...'

'Well I'm going to put him face down and stuff "offensive".'

The platoon commander hears the conversation from a few metres away, walks over and orders the corpse turned over. 'Knock it off, you blokes. He died like a soldier, and you'll bury him like a soldier.'

Later that afternoon, Dwyer was still getting over the contact and its attendant death. But his depression soon broke when a convoy of armoured personnel carriers (APCs) appeared through the trees and the platoon was told to saddle up and get on board. Climbing on to the top of a carrier, the scout knew this was another Army joke: the word was passed down that a 'Sniffer' aircraft had picked up a large heat haze using thermal imaging equipment—the haze could mean enemy. The Vietnam War was a laboratory for hi-tech weaponry. The Sniffer was an infrared contraption fitted in an aircraft that detected heat patterns beneath the jungle canopy, which could indicate groups of men present. That information was relayed to Command, who dispatched Infantry to chase the heat signature ... just in case.

That was Vietnam, Dwyer thought. *Go here, go there, no realistic plan to get the bloody job done.*

The platoon left the APCs and moved deep into the jungle. It was dark and wet, and in five minutes the men's shirts were black with sweat. One of the rifle sections headed west; Dwyer was now leading his section to the east. Somewhere out front were up to 100 VC, according to the Sniffer, but every man now strung out in single file knew they would soon bounce 100 monkeys. *Done it before, we'll do it again.* Dwyer took the bearing from his section commander and as usual picked out the thickest tree to the front— that would be his first leg before again looking back to his section commander for the next compass bearing. The forward scout carefully snipped the thicker low undergrowth with secateurs.

Step forward a few paces, swing the Armalite left and right, 180 degree arc, eyes always over the top of the rifle; who knows, the monkeys may be VC armed with AK47s.

Dwyer saw a joke in everything, but on the job as a scout he became a serious-minded individual. His philosophy regarding the war was really quite uncomplicated. *I'm a soldier, I'm a scout, and my job is to detect the enemy. Kill him before he shoots me and my mates.* But when he wasn't on the job he saw the stupid side of life, and mocked those who took the whole Army thing so seriously. Men like the platoon commander he'd had back during Infantry Training at Ingleburn. He was good-hearted, OCS Portsea, career-driven, going-to-the-top-of-somewhere. He was what one digger described as a lighthouse in the desert—bright but bloody useless. Dwyer thought he had the lieutenant's measure the day he was called on to parade outside the huts. He hobbled out, dragging his foot.

The looey spotted the hobbling Dwyer. 'Private Dwyer, you got a problem with your foot?'

'Yes sir, I've got a nail in my toe.'

Look of concern from the officer. 'Better get up to the Regimental Aid Post and get it seen to.'

'Yes sir, but I've got a nail in all my toes.'

For a second there was real concern on the officer's face, until he saw the looks on the faces of the rest of the platoon.

The looey burned for revenge against the smart-arsed digger, and got it during chopper training. Two Iroquois helicopter mock-up shells were propped up in one of the training areas; just the front sections of two choppers, no tail, no blades, no rotors. They were for platoons to practise embarking and disembarking. The soldiers would line up towards the front of the choppers and sprint forward, climb on board and take up positions on the seats. It was Mickey-Mouse training, but they were warned to enter into the spirit of it. Dwyer, always was one to get into the spirit, ran forward with the rest of his stick, ducking his head so as not to be decapitated by non-existent rotors. At the same time he made *thwoka, thwoka* noises, imitating the spinning blades. After two practice runs, the platoon commander summoned Dwyer and gave him a set of instructions. There was a protest, then a threat of disciplinary action. 'You want it more real, you'll make it more real, Private Dwyer.'

Doggy Dwyer climbed on top of the chopper shell and extended his arms, then began to spin like a ballerina.

'Can't hear you, Private Dwyer.'

'*Thwoka, thwoka,*' Dwyer did his best imitation. The rest of the trainees were by now buckling with laughter.

'Not fast enough, Private Dwyer.' The lieutenant was warming to his comedy show as the man atop the helicopter tried to spin faster.

'Can't hear you …'

Dwyer was now panting and his arms were aching. 'That's because I'm too far away now, sir … *thwoka, thwoka, thwoka …*'

There was an irritating silence. Dwyer felt the side of his face begin to tingle with numbness as he slowly moved his Armalite from the left across the front of his body—past a bush just four metres away—onto his right flank.

Hell, that was a rifle barrel sticking out of the bush!

Dwyer felt his heart sink to his kneecap. He couldn't swing back. He froze for a second, pointing away from the enemy weapon, and swivelled his eyes back.

Think quick! The next move's mine—do it right or it'll be my last.

His mind raced.

Options: keep moving as normal, maybe he wants me to pass so he can open up on the section commander behind. Or, stay where I am and swing slowly back, and when I'm level give him a full mag. Or, drop straight to the ground and spray everything with a sustained burst.

Sweat poured down his face as the scout opted to swing back. Finger now taking up the pressure on the Armalite trigger and thumb checking fire selector was on AUTO.

I can see the barrel, even the stock of the rifle. It's lowering, and the face is grinning—a big smile from an Aussie soldier.

Dwyer felt himself collapsing with the adrenaline jag. He fell to one knee. He had confronted one of Vietnam's most lethal scenarios—walking into a friendly patrol—and survived. But then his attitude towards the war, and everything in it, fell a further ten notches when he discovered he had walked in a circle back into his *own* patrol.

FEELING CROOK

By early to mid-1968, the war in Vietnam was feeding off itself, and with a voracious appetite was sucking thousands more troops and millions more tons of equipment into the conflict. More fire-power, jet aircraft, every type of helicopter and gunship, even old Dakotas—Puff The Magic Dragon armed to the gunwales. Destroyers in the South China Sea threw shells at targets deep in the jungle, and the B52 bombers flying in from Guam upped their mission count, carpet bombing and setting the country on fire from the mountains of Phuoc Tuy to the Central Highlands and all along the Ho Chi Minh Trail, the enemy's supply circuit—a camouflaged lattice of jungle trails and small roads between North and South Vietnam.

US war chief, General William Westmoreland, demanded more US troops, and pushed up the numbers in-country at any one time to 600,000. The Australian Government followed suit and shunted in a third Infantry battalion, notching up the number of Aussie ground troops at Nui Dat to 6500. Once described as a guerrilla-police action, Vietnam was now a full-blown war, with thousands of North Vietnamese Army troops pouring into the South.

February 1968 saw the enemy launch the TET Offensive: they celebrated the Chinese New Year with a massive ground assault on every town, city and military complex in South Vietnam. The vicious attacks sent the Allies into a collective nervous break-down, with real fears the South would be overrun and collapse. But the onslaught was stopped and the TET Offensive became a serious reversal for the enemy, as the North failed in its first attempt to win a complete victory on the battlefield and win over the hearts and minds of the South Vietnamese. But as '68 drew to a close, attitudes towards the war changed—certainly back home in the US and Australia. Protests began as this tele-vision war showed the dead and wounded, peasant villages in flames, and the shocking reality of B52 and napalm bombing. But what was really changing attitudes among both Americans and Australians were the number of dead and wounded coming home. A US politician had said that the war would fall from favour when the body bags started coming home to small-town America. He was right, and it was the same story in Australia.

For Ted Harrison, Trevor Lynch, Jimmy Griffiths and hundreds of other Aussie soldiers, their war was over early. 1966—Ted Harrison, a 19-year-old with shredded lungs as well as the fire and pain in his head, was already home. But his mind was still in Vietnam.

1971—Jimmy Griffiths made it home as well, but was now a bag of smashed and broken bones. Griffiths was casevaced from the bunker system in Long Khan province to an American hospital, where a medical team plastered him from the waist up, including both arms, before pumping him full of morphine. The broken veteran could recall only pain, and the gentle relief of another needle.

He was eventually flown south to Vampire, the Australian Hospital at Vung Tau, where he was strapped into a wire-and-weights world of traction. The first face Griffiths came to know as the morphine dreams passed was that of the gentle, smiling matron, Major Studholm. He recognised her from the Military Hospital at Puckapunyal. She remembered him as the soldier lout she'd thrown out of the hospital grounds for harassing her nurses. The acrimony was obviously superficial; she now sat by his bed spooning food into his mouth and writing letters for him. Like so many before him, he was eventually loaded aboard a C130 Hercules for the long flight home.

Ted Harrison felt like he wanted to die from the pain in his chest and guts; it was worse than the initial wounding. But his platoon commander told him during a hospital visit at 36 Evac that he was lucky. 'S'right, Ted, a piece of shrap smashed the grenade casing of the M26 hanging on your belt—could've blown, mate, and if it had it would certainly have cut you in half.'

Harrison was loaded on his stretcher into the back of the C130 and strapped up to the side of the fuselage wall along with other wounded. It had been suggested that the remains of Australian KIAs should also be loaded on the plane, riding along with the wounded, but there were no obvious signs to Harrison or the other patients of caskets being transported. The Hercules was not the ideal aircraft for aeromedical evacuation; arguments had long been put forward that the wounded and chronically ill should have been flown back to Australia in specially equipped chartered Boeing 707s. The problem was, such a large jet couldn't land on Vung Tau airstrip. It could fly out of Saigon, but this would involve double-handling sick men from a smaller aircraft onto a commercial airliner at Tan Son Nhut. Pressurised aircraft also presented problems to men suffering lung and head wounds. But as many diggers knew, the C130 was a hissing, rattling, almost freezing machine with an engine noise level that made talk all but impossible. Toilet facilities were primitive, and on some occasions during aeromedivac, goods and stores were slung down in the central part of the aircraft. There was no opportunity to talk in the Hercules, but a lot of time to think.

The trip home in the early years of the Vietnam War was a circuitous horror for the wounded digger. Still in political confrontation with Indonesia, the Australians could not overfly that country. So Harrison found himself on day one in the air from Vung Tau to Saigon for refuelling and then out to Butterworth RAAF air base in Malaysia. Day three was on to the Cocos

Islands and then down to Pearce in Western Australia before touchdown at Richmond, near Sydney.

Flashback: Ted Harrison—Still feeling nauseous from the pain in my chest and stomach, I'm being loaded into a long-wheel-base Land-Rover at Richmond Air Base. Destination is the Military Hospital at Ingleburn and, flat on the stretcher, I'm feeling every bloody bump and pot-hole the vehicle hits as the driver guns across town. Can't stand this shit no more.

I yell to the driver, 'Can you slow down just a bit, mate, and try missing a few of those bloody pot-holes?'

He swings around and yells back, 'Get fucked and mind your own business. I'm driving, not you.'

Later the doctors at the hospital examined Harrison and queried him closely on whether he had venereal disease. The bewildered soldier explained that he did not have VD—sadly, had never had the opportunity to contract VD—but he did have hookworm, and had dropped more than 12 kgs in weight. He was allocated a bed. With open wounds to his chest and abdomen, and unable to raise his arm above his head, the young digger struggled to tuck in the bedsheets. At 19, Ted Harrison felt isolated, alone and scared. He felt like a sick old man.

***

Wilf Matusch and the other trackers worked their way north with the platoon from Victor Company, following the Vietcong as they headed towards the Long Khan province border. The tracking dogs, Milo and Marcus, with handlers Johnno and Fergie, had held onto the VC trail like a cat on a curtain. Whenever they did wander off and were unable to lock back onto the scent pattern,

Matusch went forward and visually scanned the ground and bushes before again giving a thumbs-up to the dog handlers. There was also the smell of the enemy—that fishy-rice odour—and the occasional excrement left uncovered on the ground.

For two days the chase team headed north. The VC were not far ahead: by checking the ground-sign moisture content, Matusch determined that the patrol was just hours behind. He also figured there were up to ten of them.

The intensive tracking was wearing down all the soldiers. Principally, it was nerve-racking on super-high alert, ready for the moment Charlie might prop and set an ambush, rig a booby-trap or lead the unsuspecting Aussies into a bunker system. After 48 hours of chasing, the word came down to stop. Artillery, who had also been tracking Victor Company for the past two days, now alerted the patrol to the fact that they were out of gun range, and in the event of a major firefight there would be no assistance from the fire support base several clicks south. The patrol had also reached the Long Khan border—it was time to stop.

Every man was physically and mentally shot. Like water dripping on a stone, the war was wearing away the tough outer layers of the combatants.

It had taken him three years to get into the war. The place was York Street, Sydney on August 15, 1967 when Matusch, just 17 years and three months old, looked across the desk at the recruiting officer and listened to the spiel on becoming an officer. Matusch, a trainee metallurgist with BHP at Port Kembla, had the credentials to make Officer Training School at Portsea, but he didn't have the age. His mother, Cornelia, and stepfather, Emmanuel, listened carefully during the interview, with the officer pointing out to their son he was too young for Portsea, but not too young to be a digger.

Flashback: Wilf Matusch—The recruiting officer is coming to the peak of his sales pitch: 'You need to be 19 before we can accept you as an entrant at OCS—but, you know, with three months' recruit training, three months in a corps and 12 months in the ranks, it'll be good preparation for you.' The recruiting officer is grinning and my parents are nodding. It's pretty obvious this young officer knows what's important for my career path. He goes on: 'You'll make an excellent officer, having spent time in the ranks. You'll have real compassion for those in the ranks when you become an officer yourself.' More nods and smiles all round, then the question of length of engagement in the Army—how many years? Three or six was the norm. 'I'm here for life,' I said. 'Can I sign up for that?'

Wilf Matusch came to Vietnam as a tracker. Now he was also platoon medic. Like everything in the war, there was a shortage of trained medics. So the Infantry platoons trained up their own men to carry and use the medical kit. Matusch became platoon medic not so much by choice, but more as a result of drawing the short straw after volunteers were called for. Now he'd be responsible for patching his mates up after a fight—stem the blood flowing from wounds, wrap bandages around the busted and bleeding. It was heroic stuff, just like in the movies. He also had to dole out aspirin, ointment for crotch-rot and powder for diahorrea in the scrub. He couldn't recall ever seeing them do that in the movies.

Matusch had, in his medical role, come to notice how the men were suffering from jungle warfare: the digger who calls for a halt on patrol while he spews up his breakfast after catching the putrid smell of a decomposing corpse in a nearby enemy bunker; the soldier with a severe case of diahorrea who calls for a halt and staggers behind a bush, pulling off his webbing and trousers just in time. Then there was the soldier who stood, looking up through the trees with eyes glazed, moments before he crashed to the jungle floor with life-threatening heat stroke.

Medivac, we've got to get medivac quick or he's gone!

If the Vietnam War didn't kill or wound you, it would dismantle you piece by piece: amoebic dysentery, intestinal parasites, malaria, gastroenteritis, scrub typhus, bee and wasp stings—not to mention snakes, spiders and scorpions. Many skin diseases were ignored until they chewed deep into tissue and led to pus-filled infections. Then there were the hidden ailments—trauma, stress and anxiety. Every man in Victor Company with Matusch wore the look of the haunted, and each had shed weight to the point of almost vanishing under the loads they were lugging.

What was it that fuckwit recruiting officer said? ... Having spent time in the ranks yourself, you'll have real compassion for the men in the ranks.

THE BOYS FROM THE BUSH

Men in war band together—and unwittingly create lifelong bonds. Sometimes the bonding is in pairs, at other times trios and even larger groups, like a small football team. These men usually have something in common besides the war—maybe they come from the same town or area, maybe they like the same footy code.

From large pastoral holdings to small farms and backwater towns of nothing more than a pub, a store and a petrol station, young men from outback Australia found their path to this war—just like those who had eventually ended up at the front in World Wars I and II. Many of them were National Servicemen. To some, the war was their chance for the Big Adventure—an opportunity to escape life in the backblocks, meet new people, see the city, give military training a go, then head to war. Many took conscription philosophically; some embraced it, fervently hoping their marble would come out of the barrel so they could follow in Dad and Grandad's footsteps. There was a certain dignity and duty about all this, even if the war was in a place few had ever heard of. But then, who'd ever heard of Gallipoli before 1915?

These young Nashos got on well with Regular Army men—they certainly 'took the piss' out of each other, but they fused under fire to form competent jungle-fighting units at every level, from rifle section to Infantry battalion. These boys from the bush brought with them a rebellious streak. Many were fiercely independent, mavericks and incorrigibles who gave the Army a headache on the drill square; but you never saw a better digger when it came to a stoush. The bush soldier hated spit and polish, but he revelled in being up the front, scouting ahead of a patrol, packing an M60 or lugging the platoon's radio set. While this wasn't always the case, those who spent any time with a bunch of grunts could pick the 'bushie'.

Then there was the 'Goon Platoon'. Every battalion had the equivalent of a Goon Platoon, a combination of rebel bushies and hard-case city boys. The lethal mix was akin to Sam Peckinpah's *The Wild Bunch,* and somewhere in every Infantry unit were these problem children—the ones that had their shirts hanging out, forgot to shave, missed polishing their boots, trashed a pub in town, racked up a record of A4 charge reports. One, called 'Tailspin', had smashed up every pub en route from Sydney to his battalion posting in Brisbane. The MPs were waiting for him when he got off the train with another miscreant called 'Sparrow'. The pair had notched up enough A4s to put them in the cooler for a year, but Vietnam beckoned: Tailspin and Sparrow beat military prison, and went on to cause grief in the war zone. These men probably came from a tribe who wore their trousers back to front and flossed with barbed wire; they were tough, unpredictable and, in Army parlance, couldn't give a stuff. They sometimes had a dangerous edge, too.

Butch, Dixie, Woody and Boodgie were part of the Goon Platoon. Their Army records told something about life before the Army—but not why they scrawled 'FTA' ('Fuck The Army') on much of their equipment or how one or two of them got past the basic Army psych test. You had to love these blokes. They represented true Australian larrikinism, but you needed to be sure you were out of the way when they had a 'Yippee Shoot' in the weeds, or when they had downed an after-operation skinful back at the Dat.

Butch, an ardent surfie, was conscripted in early 1970 and thought Vietnam would be a real change from small-town jobs and a life drifting and looking for the next big wave. When his marble came out, Butch realised he'd won the first and only ballot of his life. He knew Vietnam was in Asia. The place sounded different, like it could be a hoot ... and there were lots of interesting toys to play with. He became a forward scout.

Butch loved his mates but hated the Army from day one. He

scraped through all the discipline and procedure, but made no secret of how he resented it. He was a marked man with the upper echelons, where he was quickly identified as the real thing as rebels went: a shitload of trouble ready to happen. Although short-statured, he was fearless in a fight—including with protestors in the big moratorium marches in Adelaide in the early '70s. When Butch 'went off' it was a seismic event.

He was a 20-year-old who loved a stunt, such as the one he cooked up with fellow Goons, Woody, Dixie and Boodgie to get hold of some Bacardi Rum. He was allowed to buy two bottles from the PX store so long as it was sent home and not consumed in the diggers' lines. Butch poured the rum into a water bag in his tent, refilled the 40-ounce bottles with water, had the authorisation signed by an officer, and sent them both home to Dad. Much later, the Goon Platoon laughed itself stupid at Butch's father's dark reply about the contents of the Bacardi bottles. But in the meantime a great time was had drinking the real hooch in one night's sitting.

During this booze-up Butch had a change of heart about the Vietnam War and 'went off'. In terms of mood swings, Woody and Boodgie had to admit the tantrum rated a 10. Butch sat in the tent drinking straight Bacardi from his Army-issue steel mug. 'Starting tomorrow, I'm going to make friends with Charlie.' There was a long burp followed by silence.

Woody and Boodgie thought they'd misheard their shit-faced mate. 'You talkin' about not shootin' VC?' Boodgie was on his second or third rum, and could just make out a wobbling Butch through the smoke haze under the single light bulb.

Butch drank some more and started again. 'Bloody oath. This war's got fuck-all to do with me. I got dragged into it because my bloody number came up. Chrissake, I've got no beef with Ho Chi Minh.' He pulled his rifle onto his lap and slipped off the full magazine. Woody and Boodgie stiffened while Butch went on casually cocking the action to make sure the rifle was clear: 'I made a bad mistake comin' here ... and the bloody Army ain't going to send me home. I'm fuckin' stuck here. Tomorrow I make friends with Charlie. Charlie's now my mate.'

Woody started a mild protest. 'You can't go out in the weeds with fuck-all ammo, dickhead. The Nogs'll give you a third eye before you can say "G'day, mate", that's for bloody sure ...'

Butch stood and flung his rifle magazine across the duckboard floor. He staggered over to his webbing, scrabbled through the basic pouches and hurled all his loaded magazines across the tent. They skittered under the table and the stretchers.

Woody and Boodgie sat gobsmacked, waiting for the next move. This was an unusual mood swing, even for Butch, who was now under his mosquito net snoring.

'Butch'll be back to his drongo self in the morning,' the men agreed.

Next morning, with a killer hangover, Butch readied for patrol and stumbled from his tent. Leaving all his ammunition behind, he embarked on his mission to make friends with the Vietcong.

There were no monkeys, no pigs, no elephants, no tigers. And no enemy. Doggy Dwyer and the remainder of the patrol had wandered back to the rendezvous point, where the APCs were to make the pick-up. The beat, buggered and footsore diggers had spent hours in the jungle scanning the trees and undergrowth for signs. The Sniffer had stuffed up yet again, but now there was more trouble brewing: a helicopter gunship had spotted a bunker system just a click away. The platoon got back on board the carriers for another search.

'On and off, walk, walk, walk. On and off, walk again ... it's okay for you blokes with a set of tracks.' Dwyer was trying to make conversation with the carrier commander as the machine squeaked and trundled away in convoy along the bush track, but noticed the man was agitated and preoccupied examining his map. Dwyer needed a diversion and a spot of fun after nearly shooting his own diggers. *It was the dickbrain section commander's fault, giving him an arse-up bearing.*

The diversion came in the form of the biggest unexploded bomb (UXB) the scout had ever seen—and it was straight ahead. It had partly dug itself into the ground, and was a dirty khaki colour with a yellow band around its middle. The APC groaned and swayed towards it, then the port-side track ran straight over its nose. Dwyer felt the coldness of death wash over him, then realised there was no *bang*. He pulled the APC commander over and showed him the huge shell.

'Good job we didn't run over that, might've blown a track off.' Dwyer tried to hide his grin as the tankie exploded.

'Holy Shit! Blow the friggin' track off? That'd blow half the country up!' The man was turning crimson. He pulled his map over again, running a finger across the plastic skin. Dwyer peered over his shoulder, noticing the map was covered in small chinographed red dots. 'What're they then, those dots you've marked?'

The carrier commander was sweating heavily. 'Friggin' mines that have gone off. This whole bloody area's a minefield.' The man ducked down inside the machine at the moment an explosion sounded to the front of the convoy. Black smoke shot upwards. Dwyer followed him. 'Hey mate, you still got that red pen?'

Colin Cogswell was not a mountain goat. He'd made that quite plain on the February morning when B Company was told it was humping up the mountains again. After the Nui Thi Vais and the incident with the NVA, Cogswell had seen enough of Phuoc Tuy's high country. But now the rifle company was going into the Long Hais, a stretch of mountains in the south of the province. Each soldier in the company knew this was Charlie country—the enemy were up here, and in the same numbers as in the Warbies.

After the close contact on the Nui Thi Vais, B Company's OC had congratulated the forward scout. 'A cool head in such a tense and dangerous situation—you saved a lot of lives today, Colin,' said Major Bruce McQualter.

Cogswell's machine-gunner, Joe Devlin, nudged him as they boarded the armoured carriers for the long run to the Long Hais. 'C'mon, Cogsy, you love climbing mountains. Someone told me after the Nuis that the only difference between you and a pigeon is a pigeon loves to muck about in fountains, and you love to fuck about in mountains.'

The shiaking failed to dull the anxiety that all of B Company was feeling as the carriers rumbled southwards, kicking up red dust in dry padi fields. Cogswell was travelling in the fourth machine from the front of the convoy and, squinting backwards, could just make out the face of platoon commander, Lieutenant Jack Carruthers, his big moustache covered in dust. Men pulled their sweat rags over their mouths to keep out the choking dust, and clung on as the APCs pulled out of the padi fields and began to negotiate clumps of bamboo. The carrier drivers swung through the vegetation, conscious of landmines, and then slowed as they approached a dry creek and track junction. Cogswell's instincts told him a creek and track junction was not a good place to cross ... then bang!

Flashback: Colin Cogswell—This is unreal. To his front, 11 tons of armoured carrier rises 10 feet in the air. For a moment the machine hangs suspended, surrounded by a huge orange and red fireball. One of the drive wheels is propelled 50 feet upward. The concussion and wave of heat hits, now there's black smoke, more heat and ears de-popping from the pressure. Everything's moving so slowly. Gotta do something. Pat my top pocket, where I've got the morphine syrettes, and other pockets, where I should have extra shell dressings.

I'm running with medic Doc Nicholls towards the APC.

The other APCs have turned into counter-ambush drill. Good on 'em. Smoke black, burning the throat, heat from the flames, and I'm in front of the smouldering shell of the carrier. Just visible is the top half of what's left of a soldier. The back ramp is blown clean off the machine and there are two men still inside. They look like two golliwogs from a cartoon strip, uniforms stiff and starched from the heat blast, black faces looking down at red and yellow hands, red with blood. One's looking at me with a curious bewildered expression on his face. I glance left along the side of the APC and there's an arm sticking out. Fingers aren't moving— he's dead. He wouldn't have felt any pain. There's yelling behind me. I can see Major Bruce McQualter, and other men with stretchers, running towards the shattered machine, with a look of horror on his face.

BOOM!

An invisible force picks me up and slams me down and I turn around to see other men slowly, so slowly, hugging their bodies and collapsing. Someone's screaming, 'Mines, mines.' Get up, gotta get up and help someone. I can see my mate, Barney Gee, with his hands curled up in front of his face. I pull Barney's hands down and gently prise them open. I'm looking at two slabs of mincemeat. I stand and look around—bodies everywhere, confusion and shouts mixed with pockets of silence and stupor. Gotta help Barney. Blood's pouring down my face and into my eyes. Numbness all over. Jesus, I'm full of bloody jumping jack shrap.

'Better move over a bit, Barney, I'm fucked.'

Cogswell felt someone prodding him urgently. He looked up to see the Medical Officer, Dr Tony White. 'You'll be okay, but you gotta lie still, right?' The doctor moved on to the other wounded. Cogswell slipped into unconsciousness. The jumping jack had sprung from the ground when one of McQualter's party trod on it. The main charge exploded at waist height, sending out a swathe of white-hot metal fragments. Cogswell had been buck-shot by them.

Struggling back to consciousness, he felt around his body. Then two men who looked eight feet tall were in front of him. He was lifted and half-carried and dragged between white mine-marking tape. Engineers with mine detectors had quickly sprung into action to clear safe paths along the ground to get the wounded out without kicking another mine. Cogswell realised the enormous men were some sort of visual distortion he was experiencing. As he was pushed into the dustoff chopper, he turned to see platoon sergeant 'Tassie' Wass lying alongside him. All the flesh on his arms had been shredded back to the bone; he was deathly still. Cool air washed through the aircraft passenger bay. Cogswell could just make out the coastal strip of Vung Tau coming into view, then the huge red cross on the chopper land-ing pad at the US 36th Evacuation Hospital.

ROUGH RIDERS

Wilf Matusch couldn't remember how long he'd been in-country when he tuned out to the background sounds of war: the boom of artillery, the distant sounds of small-arms fire, the incessant clatter of choppers. Everyday sounds, like traffic in a city. He'd also absorbed the stench, even got used to it. And he'd become familiar with the craziness of Vietnam—the Skull Cave, black comedy, deadpan humour. But there were still the constants that wore you down: the heat and hardship—wet or dry and shagged all the time.

Now he noticed a new sound, not unlike the screeching of brakes—a sound that announces a collision to come. Maybe it came from a fire support base, those football oval-sized locations cleared in the jungle; or perhaps from a disused rice padi, where a battery of 105 howitzers had been flown in and was now firing in support of grunts humping through the J. The ground rippled under the guns' concussion. At other times the artillery fired H and I (harassment and interdiction), another Vietnam War phenomenon whereby we dropped shells at random, day and night, on possible VC forming-up points or communication routes.

Matusch sat with a group of men, charged with the defence of the FSB, under a tree after stringing barbed wire, sandbagging machine-gun bunkers and soaking up the sounds of war. The visual tracker was having a quiet moment listening to his pocket transistor—'You've Got Your Troubles', The Fortunes from 1965; 'Baby Now That I've Found You', The Foundations, 1967; 'Cry Like A Baby', The Box Tops, 1968; 'Higher, Higher', Jackie Wilson, 1967; 'Dock Of The Bay', Otis Redding, 1968; and 'Time Is Tight', Booker T, 1969. Vietnam was Motown, rock and soul, and the sounds of a 105 letting loose in mid-afternoon.

Incoming Chinooks created small hurricanes, with their huge twin rotors sending a stream of debris in a 200-metre diameter out from the pad. The gunner hanging out of the forward port waved to the diggers as they tried in vain to shield their faces from flying grit. A piece of hessian around the latrine went flying, followed by a sheet of corrugated iron that vanished into the jungle. Later, two Hueys came clattering in—more shit, more grit. The background sound was small, super-fast Coyotes whipping over the base like something from Batman's Cave. Silence for ten minutes, then the faraway crackle of a .50 calibre machine-gun and, soon after, the short cracks of automatic weapons. Silence again, then two distant explosions that had an urgency about them: not background sound, but the sort that meant bad news. The radio operator, Alex, looked up from his set and whispered, 'Contact!'.

Was anyone dead?

Like a bird that twitches in fright with the knowledge that a gundog is nearby, the soldier shudders inwardly at a detonation that he knows signals someone's been hit. He can feel it.

The radio wasn't far from where Matusch and his mates were squatting. The news came across the net in frantic crackled messages: C Company hit by two enemy mines; two Aussies KIA. Private Dennis Neal from Queensland, a Nasho who wanted to be a motor mechanic, and fellow Nasho, bank worker, Des Tully from New South Wales, were dead. It was May 29.

The sounds of war continued: the call went out for a dustoff for the wounded. There were now more hisses and pops on the radio set—one of the dead men kept falling out of the hootchie when they tried to winch him up to the chopper. Matusch tried to picture the scenes of anguish at the death site, where men on the ground were using a plastic shelter as a make-shift sling to get the dead diggers out of the jungle.

This is sick, but what's even sicker is, it's fucking real.

More sounds from AFVN Radio: 'Hey, guys, try not to use too many tracers in your rifle. When you fire they leave deposits and may lead to jamming. Now, back to a golden hit from the Sixties, "Young Girl", The Union Gap, 1968.'

Flashback: Wilf Matusch—It's 1969 and I'm sitting with a group of soldiers in a clearing in the Bulli rainforest south of Sydney. The discussion's about dying in Vietnam. We calculate the number of dead so far, and how many real combatants are actually fighting in the jungle, and reach a conclusion. One man declares: 'Well, that makes it about a one in thirty chance of getting killed and a one in ten chance of getting wounded in a twelve-month tour. That'd be right, 'cause on average there would be one dead per platoon—and about three wounded.'

We nod in agreement with the logic.

Fire Support Base Gail was situated near Route 15, just south of a hamlet called Phu My. Route 15 snaked north from the port of Vung Tau, through the Phuoc Tuy capital of Baria and up towards the border with Bien Hoa province. It was a sealed, Vietnam-style 'highway', barely wide enough to accommodate an overloaded bus passing a truck stacked with firewood. This was the main trunk route between the southern port and Saigon. As the province was increasingly 'liberated' from the VC, an engineer team went to work repairing Route 15. FSB Gail provided the engineers' protection with its contingent of Infantry, artillery, and a support troop of Centurion tanks and APCs. But that didn't stop Charlie mining the road ahead of the engineers.

Matusch learnt this quite graphically, when he found himself the nearest available medic bent over the blast-blackened, grease-splattered body of an Australian engineer. The novice medic went into auto-pilot. *No medic's course practice on some dummy, this is bloody real.* He did everything right for the wounded soldier, who was then casevaced to Vung Tau.

Back at FSB Gail, a few days later, Matusch had things on his mind other than patching up wounded diggers: along with other platoon members, he was going for a ride on a Centurion tank. A ride on a 'Cent' sounded like a great alternative to opening a small can of ration-pack cheese, according to dog handler Johnno.

'What is this shit?' The digger nearly retched on his first bite of the guk he'd smeared on a biscuit. He read the label on the tin, squinting at the tiny writing: '"Imitation plastic cheese spread, synthetic, artificial smokehouse flavour." No wonder it tastes like shit—can't make it, they fake it.'

Matusch's section, commanded by Corporal Peter Clarke, was to 'accompany' the troop of Centurion tanks on a five-day patrol. The grunts began to look at each other darkly: grunts and 'tankies'—or 'turret heads'—always caused for some sort of stuff-up together. The 52-ton tank, some said, should never have been in Vietnam: they were monsters that got bogged in the mud, were blind in the jungle and made fabulous targets for a rocket propelled grenade (RPG). The RPG 2 could not penetrate the armour of the Cent, but the advanced RPG 7, if it struck at a perfect right angle, could burn a hole through the armour and spit burning metal fragments onto the crew. It would, however, be a brave Nog that took on the mighty tank with its awesome firepower—a super-plus advantage when engaging VC in big numbers or punching through a bunker system. Some grunts were afraid of the tank—they worried about the mess it could make of a man if it ran him over by accident in the jungle—but when it came time for a punch-up with the enemy, everyone loved the tankies and their Centurions.

Matusch and his eight companions now had to ride on the three of the monsters throughout their Infantry/Armour patrol.

'How the fuck does a tank patrol?' Matusch mumbled to his mate, Johnny Bolste, as they clambered up the back of the massive machine. It took only minutes to find out. Exhaust smoke belching from deep within the tanks quickly engulfing the three Infantrymen on the back of each one. The machines lurched and twisted, as they gave their 'passengers' a ride not unlike a Mad Mouse in a fun park. Matusch and his team hung on for their lives as the iron giants beat a run down Route 15 at nearly top speed of 35kph. Suddenly, without warning, the troop and its obligatory support vehicle, a Royal Australian Mechanical Engineer recovery APC full of spare parts and spanners, swerved east and plunged into the jungle.

'Holy shit! Slow down!' The first shouts of alarm did nothing to curb the enthusiasm of the crew: the driver, the gunner—inside with the radioman/gun loader—and the troop commander were all revelling in flattening the J at full throttle. Matusch and his two mates held on tightly to the turret; they were dragged to and fro across the vehicle as the gunner in the turret, housing the main 20-pound armament, began to swing the gun left and right, scanning the jungle ahead for enemy. The three men on the back grasped at straps and whipping radio antennae like terrified rodeo riders. The vegetation—thick branches, stalks of bamboo and thorned wait-a-while vines—swooped overhead and clawed at the helpless grunts. As the jungle thickened, a million pieces of deadfall rained down on them. Matusch heard a yell for help and twisted to see his mate, rifleman Abdul, tearing at his webbing—he managed to free himself only milliseconds before a huge bamboo stalk snagged his shirt and whipped it away with a *whoosh,* like a fish on a line.

'Stop, stop, for Chrissake, bloody *stop!*' More screams from the soldiers on the front two tanks finally brought the machines to a halt.

In the dappled jungle light, the three Centurions sat panting and gurgling amid yells of pain from two soldiers who were covered in red ants. The diggers rolled off the tank, fell and tripped over upended tree roots and broken trees as the Tank Troop commander tried to hear section commander Clarke's pleas for sanity. The tankie admitted it was his first time out with Infantry, and agreed the grunts would definitely not survive another day piggy-backing a Cent in these conditions.

One digger gave the tankies a look to kill. 'Stick this right up your bloody arse—I'm fuckin' walkin', Nogs or no Nogs.'

'Can I borrow a shirt?' asked Abdul.

The Infantry section stowed all their packs and equipment in the big bins and steel baskets on the back of the tanks, the drivers agreed to slow down, and some protocols were worked out to preserve life while riding on the Centurion. Each man who smoked immediately sucked down three cigarettes, the machines spaced out 20 metres apart, and the jungle demolition started again.

Later in the day, the rear tank got bogged in mud. Matusch climbed from the back of his machine while the recovery vehicle and its crew dragged out steel cables. The banging and clanging of men at work began to carry through the jungle. Matusch and his section found fire positions and flinched at the noise made by the turret heads as they busily worked on their tanks.

Abdul shot an anxious look into the jungle. 'Bloody Ho Chi Minh's gonna hear these fuckers in Hanoi.'

Two tanks at almost full throttle began to heave the trapped machine out of the slime. Shouts and yells came from both tank crews between the whining of 12-cylinder motors. Matusch dragged out his pocket radio, slipped the tiny earpiece in and tuned into 'Chicken Man'. *'Bock, bock, baarrck, bwaarck. Chicken Man!'*

Next moment, red-faced and breathing fire, the tank sergeant strode up. 'Hey you, dickhead grunt. You think we've stopped for a picnic? Turn that radio off, you want Charlie to hear us? We're vulnerable to bloody attack right now, you know?'

That night the Centurion troop set an ambush. The tanks backed over trees, then burbled forward and flattened the low bush to the front—like a trio of demented elephants creating a place to sleep for the night. Matusch and his section fought to keep straight faces as the tankies yelled instructions to each other—'Back up. No, forward now. Forward more. No, fuckin' forward, dumbshit. Push the bloody tree over then, dickhead!'

With the tank ambush in place, the next question was, who would be the unluckiest VC or NVA soldier in Vietnam to stroll by tonight? Sitting on a small foot track in Phuoc Tuy province were, cumulatively, three 20-pound (84mm) guns with 192 shells, three .50 calibre and three .30 calibre machine-guns with about 20,000 rounds of ammunition—and a small group of grunts who decided an uninterrupted night's sleep was quite safe.

Night came, black as squid's ink, and Doggy Dwyer prepared for night routine in the jungle. Darkness in the rainforest, with its thick overhead canopy, falls almost instantaneously. Every soldier creates his own sleeping spot. You clear away only the lumpy stuff; move too many leaves, and all the bugs and ants get pissed off and pay you back throughout the night. Next, lay out the plastic mattress cover without the blow-ups, then the silk to curl up in after you finish gun piquet. Webbing is kept near your head, with your weapon alongside it. These items are *always* in the same place. The last thing you want is to be woken by gunfire in the middle of the night and have to feel around for your equipment. In the Wet you may string the hootchie above yourself—or just curl up foetal-like and take the rain, which may fall twice in the one night.

For those with an anxious disposition or vivid imagination, night was a bad time. Best to close your eyes and listen to the chomper ants eating leaves beneath your head, think sex, think about the new car you'll get after you get home ... just don't think what's Out There.

Dwyer had barely drifted off when he was shaken awake to do two hours' sentry on the gun, the fatigue-inducing, bored-out-of-your-skull piquet. He crawled over to the M60 and found section gunner, Jim Merrin, in a half-doze. Time for a tactical smoke. Pulling a sleeping silk over his head, Dwyer lit up. He took four or five quick drags then passed it on to Merrin, who yanked the silk over his head and pulls a few quick puffs; then silk and smoke back to Dwyer.

Not far away, back at the FSB, the 105s launched an H and I mission. Three shells rushed over the soldiers' heads with that distinct freight-train *whoosh*. Moments later the rounds slam into the jungle, then the instant flash of detonation, followed seconds later by the distinct *crump! crump!*

Was some poor bastard sitting under that?

More thumps back at the FSB, more shells scream over.

Neither Merrin nor Dwyer heard the drop-short coming in— the shell that for some reason was always going to fall short of its target. Friendly fire isn't. But Merrin, always alert, already had one finger in his ear, the other over his crotch. Dwyer put both hands over his head. The shell, loaded with high explosive, detonated about 40 metres in front of the two men. A flash of bright orange, then the shockwave passed over with the distinctive *whiirr* of shrapnel. Some men were hit.

Dwyer nudged Merrin, who was peeking upwards for more drop-shorts. 'What the hell were you tryin' to protect?'

'One ear and my balls, mate.'

Flashback: Doggy Dwyer—Laying motionless in the ambush position while the mortars pound the treeline to our front. The first bombs explode very close and the eardrums pop. Next lot of mortar bombs come in—too close, too bloody close! Metal fragments rip into the bush around us. Cries of pain from the bush all around. There's a spitting sound behind me. I look around. The platoon commander has blood pouring from his mouth, where a piece of shrapnel chopped through his jaw. It almost surgically removed a molar tooth—which he is now staring at in the palm of his hand.

GRUNTS AND GOONS

The Goon Platoon's Bob 'Woody' Wood was working in the ES&A Bank in Canberra before he 'volunteered' for conscription. His birth date was not registered in the first lottery, so Wood simply called the Army and said he wanted in. The Army said volunteer properly.

Eventually he joined the First Recruit Training Battalion (1RTB), Kapooka, and single-mindedly set his sights on Infantry. Wood wanted to be a grunt. His desire to become a soldier may have had its genesis long before he became a bank clerk; at heart, the 20-year-old, who wore his hair swept back with an Elvis-style ducktail, was always a bushie. He came from a town called Dungog in the Hunter Valley, a fly speck on the map, but no youngster could have dreamt of a more wonderful place to spend his childhood. It was here that Bob Wood lived out the fantasy of the legendary Australian Light Horse. Along with his cousins, he nearly killed himself at full gallop down a 45-degree incline. In Dungog that's what horses and hills are for, and Uncle Bill and cousin Tony had a profound effect on Woody's outlook and attitudes. The two older men encouraged young Bob to take the reins and lick the face of life. Bill was a boxer, a boozer and a womaniser; Tony had been crippled by polio during his Army service and walked with a stick. But before he was afflicted with the disease that sent him home to help his sisters and mother run the dairy farm, Tony had already taught young Bob how to hunt, track and skin animals. Around campfires at night, the older man mentored the boy in the ways of life in the bush.

Flashback: Bob Wood—A campfire in the scrub near the Hunter Valley. Tony leans over and speaks softly, 'Be alert and relaxed at the same time. Remember, with foxes, dingoes and 'roos, you only get one shot. You must be ready to take it, and make the first shot count.'

Bob Wood and his fellow Goons from 7 Platoon, Charlie Company, 3RAR—Butch, Dixie and Boodgie—were finding that in this so-called 'helicopter war' they seemed to be walking a lot. In fact, it was day four on operations in-country and they all felt frustrated and exhausted with the sauna-like heat of Phuoc Tuy and the lack of action. They collectively considered they were in a bullshit war. There was definitely not a Vietcong in sight; no-one in the battalion had shot a Nog yet, not even a *bang* to get a rush going in the first week of walking in the weeds. Although, they had to remind themselves, this first week in Vietnam was what the Army commanders called 'in-theatre training.'

The Goons were on a search and destroy mission; thus far it had been more search and avoid, wheeze and spit, scratch and curse in the jungle. They were told that the enemy was definitely ahead of them—somewhere. The hours dragged by, sweat sluicing down backs. Shortly before dark, they broke out into a clearing of waist-high grass and thick clumps of tall bamboo. The platoon commander called for a night stop, and the diggers went into a circular harbour, machine-guns covering the thick vegetation across the clearing. Not far away, on the other side of the dense bush, Delta Company had also gone into night harbour. The men were still preparing for night routine when three Centurion tanks rumbled up and placed themselves around the outside of the harbour—one directly in front of the Goons.

'Not happy, mate,' said Woody. 'Sarge says if the shit hits the fan tonight, that bloody Cent'll draw Nogs and a shed-full of RPGs like the crabs.'

Night came. The mites, mosquitoes and other bugs with jaws like wire-cutters had already found the dozing soldiers when the enemy attacked Delta Company.

Flashback: Bob Wood—The night turns to a deafening red, yellow and orange smoke-filled 'day' as the Claymore mines, set in front of the Australians to repel a mass attack, detonated in banks of three at a time. Darkness, then a flash of yellow. Blackness, then bright lights like a set of strobes when a wall of Australian automatic fire erupts around the edge of the bamboo, tracers almost lazily marking the path of the rounds into the surrounding bush. Get up near the tank and take up a fire position. They'll probably come across the open ground when they have a go at us. Breathing quick, shallow, too loud. First contact in war, and the first sensation is energy-draining terror. Then a peace comes over me and a voice is speaking quietly. It's my mother, whispering to me that it'll be all right, nothing will happen to me. Like a guardian angel …

Night fights are situations of fundamental confusion, with flashes of muzzle fire, the fiery trail of a rocket, the dazzling burst of an explosion, orders shouted through the blackness. *What's going on? How many? Which direction, which bloody direction?*

A main force enemy group, platoon size or larger, had hit D Company. The attack seemed to go on for hours, and the sounds of battle—automatic bursts of gunfire and explosions—carried across to the Goon Platoon. Woody heard the crackle of gunfire in the distance, then two loud explosions. Delta Company Platoon Commander, Lieutenant John Wheeler—in Vietnam less than a week, and the grandson of an original Anzac—was killed, along with Paul Manning, a former Infantry rifleman and police cadet.

Beneath the dry bamboo, Woody and his mates watched, mesmerised, as Aussie Iroquois gunships wheeled out of the night and sent streams of mini-gun fire and rockets into the jungle along the corridor between the two rifle companies. Like two giant iridescent red snakes, the firepower reached down along the ground as streams of bullets were pumped at 6500 rounds per minute. Then a flash like lightning and a *crack-boom* sound that almost blew in the eardrums and sent an electric shock down the spine. It took a moment to realise that one of the Centurions had opened up with its main armament, firing a canister round which turned the thick bush to its front into coleslaw.

To the Australians it all lasted mere minutes. Maybe it really was hours—but the fight finished with astonishing suddenness, and then there was only the crackle of sitreps over the radio set. Now silence, as smothering as the blackness in the bamboo. Men slumped or lay on their stomachs and stared into the coalpit. Not one soldier slept that night. The first taste of combat had been surreal, a series of flashes, explosions ... and not a glimpse of the enemy.

In the morning the Goons crept cautiously across the battleground searching for dead VC. No enemy bodies, no flesh or blood, just one solitary Vietcong rubber sandal. The message came down the line later that day: 'The training's over.'

Bob Wood prided himself on his bushcraft. Thanks to cousin Tony, he felt he had a compass built into his brain and an intuitive knack for reading landscapes. During a training exercise at the Infantry Centre near Singleton, Wood's platoon commander had become lost and, with a storm approaching, Wood led the platoon out of the hills. But his internal compass sometimes swung away from Magnetic North. Not long after the first night attack on Delta Company, the Goons, still jumping up and down inside their skins, were pushing hard towards a suspected VC camp when darkness caught the platoon and the soldiers went into another quick harbour. Wood and Boodgie were pushed forward into a two-man firing position near a large tree on an incline in the thick bush. The remainder of the platoon—set in a bamboo clump back from the Wood-Boodgie duo—completed the circular harbour.

Shortly after stand-down the world turned black. There was a probe by the VC that night, and the Goons had what they thought was another firefight on their hands. Wood and Boodgie shot bolt upright as the first shots were fired. The two mates seized their weapons and sent a burst of automatic fire back at the muzzle flashes.

'These bastards are layin' it on, mate,' said Wood after almost emptying his magazine in one long burst. 'Eat that, mongrels!' Flinching at the amount of lead whipping above his head, he added, 'Must be a friggin' battalion of the fuckers.' It was only when Wood turned to his mate that he noticed the large tree was now behind them instead of in front. He nudged Boodgie, who was going through an immediate-action reload. 'Boodgie, has that tree moved? Wasn't the bloody thing to our front an hour ago?'

Before his mate could answer, more rounds cracked over their heads. Boodgie snapped on another 20-round magazine. Both men then looked at the tree again—the tree that was earlier providing them with cover to their front.

Boodgie: 'Nah, bullshit ... '

Woody: 'Yeah, bloody oath ... Shit, mate, we're firing the wrong fucking way.'

Like a scene from 'Dad and Dave', both men quietly spun around and fired into the darkness behind them, just as the platoon sergeant, on hands and knees, scrambled down the slope to the two men.

'Hell, you bastards okay? There's a shitload of fire coming from down here.'

Wood drew in a breath, cleared his throat and tried to stifle a cough. 'Yeah, s'okay, Sarge, we got their bloody heads down an' they've moved away to the left.'

In the darkness and silence that followed, the two men argued on. 'Bugger it, Boodgie, next time before you go to sleep, get a fucking landmark, will ya?'

Four weeks on, and a quiet afternoon in the jungle. It was like the war had shut down for the day; even the drone of choppers had gone. The platoon worked hard all morning: patrol, stop, move, patrol, prop, listen, smoke. They seemed to be doing what Infantry soldiers complain about in all wars: walking around in circles, hoping to bump the enemy. The Vietcong did the same, hoping to bump the Australians. Enter the afternoon heat, and the Goons collapsed in a defensive perimeter for a lunch break. The bush was quiet, almost welcoming the band of men now sitting cross-legged, packs off, munching biscuits and cheese and brewing coffee among clumps of vine and bamboo.

The Goon Platoon, like every Infantry unit before it, was now discovering what real war meant to the soldier; its members were bonding as only men in war can. The rites of passage might involve punching the suitcases out of each other after a gutful in the boozer, arguing and slapping each other around over a card game and illegal piss-up in the tents at Nui Dat, and detecting each other's weaknesses but never exploiting them beyond good-humoured banter. The Army 'constructed' each soldier to fit its mould; on the surface it seemed that way, but each man remained so unlike the next. The Army scoured out individuality—it wanted teams, teams of men who would act instinctively—but it would never scrub out the characters.

The men sat in pairs as they caught their breath. They were unshaven, they stank and wore torn and filthy greens; parade-ground presentation didn't matter out here. Each man automatically took up a fire position and searched his arc of responsibility: watch the front, peer into the gloom, look for the enemy. Look out for your mates and they'll look out for you. The bonding went further. You got to know a man so well you could immediately recognise his personal gear. Wood reckoned he could identify his mates in the section just by their boots, their backpacks—by the way a piece of hootchie cord held an extra water bottle in place—or even by the individual length of a sweat rag around a man's neck.

Jesus, it's like being married to one of the ugly bastards. We're just a bunch of Nashos—no-hopers, bank clerks, country yokels and surfies like Butch, who keeps in training by throwing himself down in the Nui Dat mud and surfing on his guts. But who ever knew a greater bunch of blokes …

Bob Wood knew at that moment why he'd become an Infantryman: it represented the ultimate in trust. You placed your life in the hands of another man. If he stuffed up, you were dead. And if you missed the first sign of VC, Dixie or Boodgie could be dead. Another aspect of this mateship was beyond the I-preserve-him-he'll-preserve-me factor: almost without exception, each man had become totally unselfish towards his mates. Each Goon could almost read the others' thoughts: stop for an extra minute if it looked like his mate was buggered; lift an extra link belt of ammo from a soldier's back if he was doing it hard. During a break, Dixie was making two brews—one for himself and one for Woody—while Wood rummaged in his pack and prepared two packets of biscuits and two small cans of fruit. You always tossed your packet of smokes to a mate after you'd lit up. Everything was done by the 'buddy system'.

By the fourth week, every digger knew that when it came to 'Deep Serious', the man behind would always be up alongside you. These things have always happened with Australians in war. *And they probably always will*, thought Wood in the silence of the afternoon.

Flashback: Bob Wood—Kapooka, First Recruit Training Battalion. Like dealing with an errant child, the Corps Allocation Officer is struggling to be patient with me. 'Recruit Wood, you have three choices of corps after completing training here. You have nominated Infantry in all three boxes. Do it again.'

Time to put on the best Bob Wood dumbshit act: 'Aah, sorry Sir, I think I've got it now—next to the first box I put first choice, second box my second choice and third box, my third choice?'

Officer, nodding his head and growing more irritated: 'Correct, now mark them again on this new sheet.'

The officer goes red and bites his lip with frustration. He stares at me like I'm something stuck to his shoe, then back down at the sheet of paper with the new allocation choice, which reads:

1. Infantry.
2. Infantry.
3. Infantry.

Bob Wood Rule of Life: Bullshit baffles brains.

SHOCK WAVE

The three dustoff Hueys appeared as dots in the east. They banked to the south-west and, with the pilots stretching the limits of their machines, thundered just above the surf of the South China Sea, heading towards the Australian hospital at the First Australian Logistics Support Group (1ALSG), Vung Tau. The American dustoffs, with the red cross emblem emblazoned on each side of the fuselage, were named by their crews—*Doctor Copter*, *Band Aid Special* and *CC-Rider*, the nomenclature revealing their vital role in the war.

Colin Cogswell, still losing blood, drifted in and out of consciousness. He didn't hear the wail of the World War II air-raid siren at Vampire warning of incoming wounded. The howling siren never failed to stop the ALSG-based soldiers dead in their tracks: they shielded their eyes and looked up and out along the sandy coastal strip for the racing helicopters, each man thinking, *Who's the poor bastard that's got it now? Thank fuck it's not me.*

The medical staff were ready in no time: they went into a well-practiced drill as the dustoffs radioed ahead their manifest of KIA, those on litters, those serious, and any soldiers still ambulant. By the time the first chopper touched down, stretchers and wheelchairs were ready, and a medical orderly carefully took the still-loaded weapons from the walking wounded. This was a dangerous, unpredictable task—some men, eyes still spinning like those of a terrified horse, had been in combat just minutes before, and were 'out of it' with fear and suspicion. There was always the possibility that, due to profound shock, they may open fire. The weaponry, including hand grenades, flares and even Claymore mines, was dropped into a sandbagged pit to be later cleared by the Engineers. But the wounded soldier knew that if he made Vampire—he'd make it home. Cogswell felt himself being gently lifted out of the Huey. There were smiling faces looking into his, whispers, then his clothes were cut away.

Flashback: Colin Cogswell—People running everywhere, then I'm on a cool, stainless-steel table, stark naked. Drips in my arm and up my nose. Why don't they stick one in my bum? Darkness again.

Now there's a man yelling and abusing the nurses, screaming in pain.

Wheeling me into an operating theatre. Whispers of reassurance. 'You'll be right, mate, you're in good hands.'

No pain yet. Other men are being operated on already, one each side. Dark in here, dark all around except for those bright lights above. Feel good. Feeling safe.

Some of the best surgeons in the world spent five hours on Colin Cogswell. The scout had taken two pieces of shrapnel in his head, and three in his back and chest; his arm and leg were also impregnated with pieces from the jumping jack.

'There are fragments elsewhere in your body but we'll take those out later,' he was told. Inevitably, the pain came, but to Cogswell, his stay at Vampire was made bearable by the treatment from the most compassionate and caring people he'd ever met in his short life. All his wounds were left open, with tubing criss-crossing his torso to hold his stomach in. The surgical protocol in Vietnam was to leave the wounds open and pack them with gauze until the patient arrived back in Australia: the combination of humidity and dirty shrapnel could lead to gangrene if the wounds were closed up.

```
SALISBURY SOUTH AUSTRALIA
MRS. L B COGSWELL
REMOVED FROM SERIOUSLY ILL LIST STOP IT IS
LEARNED WITH PLEASURE THAT YOUR SON 43755
PRIVATE COLIN JOHN ROYSTON COGSWELL NOW
LOCATED AT 2 CAMP HOSPITAL INGLEBURN NEW SOUTH
```

WALES HAS BEEN REMOVED FROM THE SERIOUSLY ILL
LIST AND IS PROGRESSING SATISFACTORILY STOP
FURTHER INFORMATION REGARDING HIS TRANSFER TO
HOSPITAL IN ADELAIDE WILL BE ADVISED IMMEDI-
ATELY IT IS RECEIVED—ARMY HEADQUARTERS

Two days' butt-breaking ride on the Centurions, and Wilf
Matusch had seen and heard sufficient of the Royal Australian
Armoured Corps to last him the rest of his military career. The
troop had knocked down enough rainforest to print a million
newspapers, had sent every living creature scurrying for its life,
and had effectively cut a swathe big enough for a motorway
through some of the thickest J in Phuoc Tuy.

No sign of enemy—Charlie would have to be tooled up with
some pretty serious ordnance to take on the tankies. But there
was disquieting news on the Vietcong and the NVA: July, 1970,
and the war was cranking up again—contact, ambush, bunker
fight. The transmissions coming over the network sent a prickle
across the scalp and kept the nerves zinging along in overdrive.
Despite the black carnival the Infantry were enduring on tank
patrol, not one man switched off. When the machines ground to
a stop late in the afternoon of the second day, the men quietly
went about making a brew. A radio man on a nearby Cent
snapped his fingers and spoke urgently: 'Kiwis are in contact with
three Victor Charlie—one VC WIA.'

Another burst of transmission came over the radio static, then
more sitreps. 'One VC now KIA.'

The radio operator looked puzzled. 'The Nog's died and someone said something about evening up a score.'

Matusch smiled—Kiwi Roly from Victor Company was still in

the thick of things. More fidgeting with the radio, more crackle of automatic fire, then bad news. 'Aussie contact—it sounds like Alpha Company … both Sunrays have lost their feet just above the ankle.' Platoon commanders—Sunrays—had fallen victim to mines and booby-traps.

Silence. Those who smoked dug about in their packs for one. Others just stared into the trees.

Just after 1100 hours on day three, the tanks and their passengers found the real war again. The men on the Centurions could see a group of low hills to the west: like a dozen eyes winking, there were small, soundless flashes of orange mushrooming across the hazy jungle-covered slopes, followed by clouds of black smoke. Heavy artillery pieces from nearby were pounding VC caves and tunnels.

The troop broke cover, knocked down the last of the thick vegetation and rumbled out onto the Firestone Trail. This was a massive freeway of flattened trees that crossed the province east-west. The Firestone was the largest of the fire trails cut through the jungles of Phuoc Tuy: it was as wide as a four-lane highway. Removing cover and denying the enemy criss-cross access within the province, the fire trails were bulldozed by tractors called Rome Ploughs, protected by Infantry and armour during the demolition job. It also gave access to future Allied Force operations, allowing tanks and mobile guns to traverse the cleared areas. But the enemy turned this to his advantage, creeping onto the trails under cover of darkness and planting dozens of mines and booby-traps. Five American mobile guns were positioned on the trail; they ignored the Australian Centurions now motoring across it. Suddenly there was a *flash–bang* and the 155mm juggernaut—a cross between a tank and a huge howitzer—jerked backwards, hurling a shell into the hills. Then another shell went on its way, followed moments later by an orange wink on the hillside and a dull crump.

'This is some serious sort of shit.' Abdul nudged Matusch and pointed to the far side of the clearing, where another piece of war technology was hurling lead and fire at the enemy. The 'Duster' consisted of four .50 calibre machine-guns or twin 40mm bofors mounted on a tracked armoured vehicle. Several of them were sending sheets of fire into the hills.

That's the war, Matusch thought to himself, *lots of big, lethal machines that make really big bangs.* Near the Dusters was an APC, but Matusch's attention was caught by a lone Duster with a group of black American soldiers on top who were giving the Australians raised clench fists.

'Black Power salute,' said Matusch, pumping his arm up and back at the Americans. The black soldiers raised their fists again and shouted. The Australians responded with two fingers up. A moment later the lead 52-ton Centurion ran over an antipersonnel mine. The charge was small, and the damage akin to a car blowing a tyre, but it was enough of a shock to send the Aussies into high alert, fingers tightening on rifle pistol grips. The Australian mechanical engineer from the Royal Australian Electrical and Mechanical Engineers (RAEME) vehicle bent and looked at the damage. 'Broken track. That wasn't the Black Power salute. They were telling us we're in a minefield. Must think we're king-size dickheads.'

Carefully walking in the tanks' track treads over to the Duster, Matusch and his fellow grunts found that its rolling gear and tracks had been blown away. It had hit a much larger landmine. The Australians offered the Duster and crew a tow to Highway 15. The offer was accepted, so the Cent hooked up a steel line for a 'skull drag': the Cent pulled the Duster on its belly along the sand and mud of the Firestone Trail.

At times like this, combatants became mechanics, like boys hanging around the local legend who is pulling his engine to pieces—lots of advice and suggestions, and at the same time a chance to say 'G'day' and 'Hi buddy, how much time you got?' and 'What the goddamn hell you doin' in this sorry-arsed place?'

The fire mission blasting the mountain was over, the big 155s were packed up for the day and the convoy clanked and squeaked west to Highway 15. Matusch sat on the drag tank. The two other Cents were taking the lead, and the mobile 155 guns pulled up the rear behind the disabled Duster. Matusch, Abdul and Theo watched the sand being pushed ahead under the damaged belly of the Duster with its crew sitting on top. It was like watching a bunch of skiers.

Blink! You've missed the sand beneath the Duster exploding upwards. Then the crack of the huge detonation as the Duster hit a mine. The wall of heat and the shockwave hit the men on the back of the Centurion, blowing them away like tissue paper, while the Americans on the Duster were thrown into the air and across the back of the machine.

'We've been hit! We're being ambushed!' The tank crew commander screamed to the men in the machines in front and the troop went into contact drill, swinging the turrets of the main guns left and right. The grinding sound Matusch and the soldiers heard, while prostrate in the mud and checking their limbs were still intact, was an Australian digger's Armalite being ground into a mangled mess beneath the swinging gun turret. The tank commander jumped down from his machine as the first ammunition boxes exploded inside the Duster. The tankie unhooked the steel cable and yelled at his driver to get going. Matusch and the other diggers panted and ran after the Centurion like dogs chasing a car, trying to get a purchase on the back ramp to pull themselves back on board to retrieve their weapons.

'Anyone hit, anyone hurt? Any blood? All okay?' Matusch checked his mates, faces blackened by the blast and just white eyes staring out—*Hell, we look like hopefuls in the 'Black and White Minstrel Show'*.

More bangs from the Duster, with more ammo boxes catching fire and exploding while tracers zipped through the air. The tank commander yelled down at the Infantrymen who were still checking for wounds. 'Medic, we need a medic! Have we got one?'

Matusch put his hand up, 'Yeah, here …'

'Two or three Yanks have been hit, I'm calling in a dustoff. Get down there and see what you can do.'

Matusch began to make his way towards the smoking wreck. He heard the tankie call out from behind him, 'Watch your bloody step. Tip-toe, we're in a minefield.'

He swung off the tanks' track treads into the shoulder-high elephant grass. *Fuck this, I'm getting off the track and into the grass. I'm a visual tracker, I'll know if any bastard's put mines in here*. It was the longest, loneliest 300-yard walk of his life, tip-toeing, fully aware of the terror of hearing that distinctive metallic click.

The wounded Duster crewman was going into shock. Matusch felt the clammy body and determined that an arm was broken. His pulse was racing as fast as the American's, and it jumped a notch when he heard the dustoff droning in. Men were struggling to get the wounded American into a tarpaulin to carry him to the aircraft. *Bugger it*. Matusch lifted the wounded man in both his arms and ran to the chopper.

Later that night the Centurions went into their night harbour position, called a 'liger', and the Infantry settled down, watching the shadows lengthen on the Firestone. Theo examined his buckled Armalite. 'What the fuck do I do now, in a war zone without a fire-stick? I might as well be in the main street of Brisbane stark naked.'

Theo was dissuaded from test-firing his weapon once he was

informed of the likelihood of it blowing up in his face. So he set out on his embarrassing walk around the Centurions looking for a spare rifle, one that wouldn't shoot around corners if it didn't first explode. Matusch had barely drifted off into a fitful doze when the tanks opened up with canister rounds. The splinters ripped into the jungle on both sides of the trail, and the *crack* and echoing *boom* seemed to erupt inside Matusch's head, sending him into severe post-traumatic shock.

Overload! Nerves shredded. You go into the twilight zone during sleep, where the mind replays the traumas of the day. Next second you are wide awake, reaching for your rifle. There is a flash of bright yellow. Panic, a second of terror, and you feel the concussion lift you from the ground ...

Flashback: Wilf Matusch—Can't breathe, can't speak, arms thrashing. A soldier jumps on my chest, puts a hand over my mouth. 'You're okay, Wilf. Wilf! You're okay, stop struggling.' Can't breathe, rivers of sweat coursing down my body. Another soldier holds my arms, pinning me down.

Later that night the panic attack subsided. Matusch's mates urged him to breathe slowly, deeply. They considered calling in a dustoff to take him out, but he was talked into a state of relative calm. He ceased hyperventilating and, as a group, the soldiers whispered quietly through the night, sucking on a tactical smoke every ten minutes.

RULES OF ENGAGEMENT

Rule One in the jungle war against the Vietcong was the Rule of Engagement: if in doubt, don't fire.

Bullshit, thought Doggy Dwyer. *One black shape too many and they get half a magazine of tracer down their throat. If in doubt, empty the magazine.* Another Rule: never walk on tracks and trails, they may be mined or booby-trapped. *Right,* thought Dwyer, *that's why I'm walking through shit I can hardly see in next to a perfectly good foot track.* The forward scout had been doing his scouting by the book, carefully cutting his way with secateurs alongside the foot track, when he heard a distinctly metallic sound above him.

A Rule Not Yet Revealed: beware of unexploded bombs falling from trees onto your head.

Dwyer felt his heart somersault as he watched the unexploded cluster bomb shake loose from the vines above and land a metre from his boot. The American cluster or 'butterfly' bombs were, in fact, bomblets released from a canister in the air. They hit the ground and peppered the enemy with numerous small explosions. Dwyer stared at the small winged bomblet, then turned and held his hand, open palm up with fingers pointing to the sky, indicating to the section commander mine or booby-trap.

'I'm gonna have a word with the Yanks about their quality control after this,' said Dwyer while the section commander examined the UXB. 'That bugger should've gone off when it hit the ground just then.'

The section commander gave the scout a sharp look. 'You okay, Doggy? You wanna talk to a Padre or something ...?'

Hours later the scout collapsed for a breather. It had taken a while, but now the full impact of the brush with the bomblet was sinking in. *That's Vietnam—nearly killed or chopped into small pieces, and we carry on like absolutely fuck-all's happened.*

The war was hard, harder than Canungra and a hundred times harder than anyone in the platoon had expected. It chipped away at them in a thousand small ways—regular drenchings, the load on the back, the sick feeling in the guts from unrelenting tension, the lack of sleep, the all-day exhaustion—which got to them incrementally. Never had Dwyer felt so tired. For four days the platoon had been patrolling and laying ambushes at night, and everyone was so buggered, they could hardly speak. Every soldier was becoming an automaton, a potentially lethal state of mind in any sort of warfare. Some of the men talked of shooting themselves, busting a leg, throwing on a vomiting fit, anything, anything to get out of the jungle. Anything to lie down and sleep ... give in to total, black unconsciousness for just one day.

And, burning up thousands of calories a day, the situation was exacerbated by the fact that they had two mealtimes to go before resupply and everyone was already out of food. Worse still, intelligence indicated a heavy enemy presence in the area, so there would be no chopper resup. Dwyer ran his hands over his face—he hadn't shaved for a week. He looked at his greens; they weren't green any more, they were dry slime painted onto his skin. 'The baggy green skin.' His hands were raw from bush work—as scout he had to choose the route cautiously, cutting through the thick stuff. This resulted in almost every piece of exposed skin being ripped or stained with dry blood. The razor grass and wait-a-while vine turned a grunt's life into a walking hell.

There was nothing clean, orderly or precise about war; nothing neat and surgical. To start with, you never saw the enemy. The NVA soldier, in his green uniform and pith helmet, could be watching you now. The Vietcong, in his black uniform, could be quietly moving into an ambush just ahead of you in the jungle.

Dwyer was wondering if he really cared any more, anyway. Anything that would for just a moment allow him to explode, to blast the hell out of anything or anyone! Chicken de-beaking was looking really good right now. The anger rose in his throat until he could taste it like bile. The one person he really wanted to shoot was the bastard who'd refused the ration resupply. The scout pulled his pack over and scrabbled around in a sidepocket for something to eat. Eight sugar cubes. He crawled back to the thee-man group immediately behind him and quietly shared the pitiful sustenance with his mates.

Next day, still no rations and more aggravation: a group of ten Vietnamese were chattering, smiling and gesticulating, but they smelt very much like enemy.

'All in black and I'm telling you, one of the bastards in front had a friggin' weapon.' Doggy Dwyer was whispering urgently to his section commander. 'Rules of bloody engagement? Shoot the bastards and who's going to know the friggin' difference? This mob is Charlie, mate, I'm tellin' you. They've accidentally walked straight into us and have hidden their weapons in the trees.'

Dwyer was still muttering his suspicions when the platoon commander strode up with a Vietnamese Bushman Scout. These scouts, usually ex-Vietcong who had defected, were used by Australians on patrols to interpret and gain information about possible enemy movement from the villagers. That's what was happening now—finding out who the men were and where they had come from.

'Escort them back to their village, right? So the buggers can have another go.' Dwyer echoed the sentiments of the others in the platoon as they moved off for the 500-metre walk to the village. Not far from the hamlet, in a rubber plantation, the forward scout nearly had a heart attack as the Vietnamese he had his rifle trained on stopped and began to move away from the main group.

'Hey, you back here, back here!'

Dwyer moved his rifle barrel to indicate the direction. The man turned and looked at Dwyer, and smiled—then bent down.

'Jesus, fuck ...' the scout thumbed the selector on the Armalite to AUTO and watched transfixed as the man began to lift from the grass an object with a long wooden stock.

'Stop, fucker, I'm gonna shoot ...'

The man continued to slowly lift the object.

It's a bloody rifle. 'Stop *now!*' Dwyer pulled his weapon back into his shoulder and took the first pressure on the trigger.

This is not happening. I've got to kill him! Clean shot to the head, now! The Vietnamese smiled and stood erect with a machete-like banana-cutter in his hand, then walked towards the rest of his group, still smiling at the scout. Dwyer felt all the energy rush from his body; at the same time his mind was flooded with life's 'what if's. *What if I had fired? What if it was an AK-47 and he came up putting a burst into me? What if I had killed him and he was found with the bloody banana-cutter? What if I was court-martialled for not following the rules of engagement? What if I had stayed home in Badgery's Creek? What if my aunty had been born with balls? What if I had never heard of the fuckin' Army? Too many 'what if's. Just get me out of this place.*

Alice Harrison was looking at her teenage son—19 years and eight months old, and now a sick 'old' man. She could see that the fire in Ted Harrison's eyes had gone out, his spontaneity vanished. He used to be so quick with a quip, but no more; the shutters had come down.

Alice had already gone through the anguish of all mothers whose sons have gone to war—the daily agony of uncertainty; the lack of communication, except Ted's letters and newspaper reports that carried snippets from the war zone:

AAP: Australian troops were involved in heavy action against

VC in Phuoc Tuy province this week. Australian casualties were described as light …

The telegram announcing his wounding had sent her into a breakdown, but she had composed herself sufficiently to take Ted home after the doctors had done all they could at 2 Camp Hospital.

Ted Harrison now sat on the side of his own bed. It was 2 a.m. and his mother quietly walked up the hallway to check on her boy. She looked in and saw what the Army called a 'light casualty': a young man slumped over with his arms wrapped around his body, panting with the pain in his stomach. And there was something wrong in his head.

He sat in the dark and recalled the medical staff telling him that some soldiers who came home after they'd been wounded spent all night and day with the lights switched on. Harrison thought that sounded a bit silly. His foot bumped something solid under the bed—a pick-handle. He hadn't told anyone he'd put it there.

When you think about a bloke who has to try and sleep with a pick-handle under his bed, that lights-on story didn't sound so stupid any more.

He wasn't game to stash a .22 rifle under there. There was sometimes this irrational thought that he may use it … on himself.

MANNA FROM HEAVEN

An Iroquois landing in a jungle clearing with a resupply of rations and equipment is a storm of flying dust, bamboo leaves, grit and twigs. The soldiers, kneeling on the edge of the clearing, pull sweat rags over their faces or a bush hat over their eyes to block out the waves of debris. They hope the aircraft will leave before Charlie wises up to the racket and comes a'calling with a big hello.

Resupply day was always a good day as far as the diggers were concerned—it meant less walking, more rest, and goodies from the sky. This was the one day in the weeds when the entire Company came together, which gave everyone the opportunity to catch up with mates in the other platoons. The resup chopper—that most wonderful of sights—also meant replacement webbing, spare parts for the M60, a new Armalite to replace one that malfunctioned, and new jungle greens for shirts and trousers falling apart from wear, tear, water and mud. There were combat rations and supplementary packs, more smokes, cold cans of drink (called 'goffas') and chocolate-flavoured milk. There were fluffy white bread rolls stuffed with ham and lettuce, prepared by the company cooks back at the Dat. Manna from Heaven. *God bless the tuckerfuckers.* And there was a mailbag with letters from home—good and bad news, but at least some contact with the Real World.

The platoon sergeant was shouting orders at the Goons while the resup chopper wobbled and jerked in an effort to get off the ground; the pilot, with one hand on the cyclic stick and the other twisting the throttle grip on the end of the collective stick, cautiously swung through 180 degrees. Its nose went down and the Huey raced towards the edge of the clearing, then lifted and hedge-hopped across the bamboo. The clatter became a hum, which soon turned to a drone. Silence returned to the jungle like a radio twisted from loud to mute.

'Come on. Get moving—Woody, get your bloody hand outta that mailbag.' The sergeant was The Man when it came to resup. The platoon commander, Lieutenant Dennis Tyson, ran the show, but the bloke with three stripes ran the resup and the collection and distribution of the goodies. Men swung sandbags over their shoulders and lugged the cardboard cartons of rations and supplementary packs and water bladders back into the cover of the trees.

With the roar of the chopper long gone, the soldiers reverted to whispers, almost like they weren't really on the side of the LZ; as if the resup had never happened. The sergeant quietly continued his harassment, well aware of the urgent need to get back to a tactical status.

'Woody, get out of those shit clothes and get new greens on— that's what you bloody asked for, wasn't it? Dixie, mail for you.' A letter was shoved into the soldier's hand as the sergeant continued to work his way around the men, handing out the letters.

Men were pulling off their filthy sweat-soaked rags. They were prising apart supp packs, tossing around White Owl cigars, packets of Marlboro and Kool, Hershey bars and sticks of chewing gum, even cans of Smooth shaving cream. Into holes that had been hastily dug went the rubbish: chewing tobacco, cardboard and boots that had been ripped and split during patrols. Many men were lying on the ground, resting, leaning back against their packs, slumped sideways against a convenient tree, hats tilted forward, scoffing the fresh bread rolls, eyes racing across the pages of their mail with a grin or a grunt.

A soldier prodded Dixie's foot. 'I got two letters this week, Dixie. Told me she loves me.'

Dixie shook out his letter. Cartoon strips cut from newspapers fluttered out: 'Dagwood', 'Ginger Meggs', 'The Potts' and three crossword puzzles.

The cartoon strips were passed around to men who hadn't received any mail. It was a silent process that needed no explanation—a bloke had to have something to read. One digger rushed from section to section, proudly displaying a tuft of his girlfriend's blonde hair, others sniffed their mates' perfume-soaked letters.

Boodgie was kicking Woody's boot. 'Come on, you slack bastard, you've read that bloody letter twice. What's happening back in the world—they still callin' us "baby killers"?'

Occasionally a 'Dear John' letter arrived, and for the sergeant this was always a time of anxiety, an occasion he hated: it didn't just mean he had to deal with the grief that followed, but had to watch that word didn't spread too far among the troops that some bloke's girl had flicked him. This could have a poisoning effect, giving other diggers the idea that their relationships may also collapse.

The sergeant supervised the last of the resup distribution, saw that all was well again with the war, and quietly walked out to the LZ to recover the now cool and blackened smoke canister he had earlier tossed to mark the spot for the pilot. While walking back, he heard a commotion, and looked towards the platoon to see Butch covered from head to foot in shaving cream. The soldier, a grin spread across his face, flapped his arm like a happy pelican white balls of cream flying in all directions.

Flashback: Dixie—A heavy night of contact with the VC and the resup comes in next morning with a load of ammo. The pilot drops towards the low grass in front of our position and the Company Quartermaster, Reg French, begins kicking sandbags of ammo out. Uh-oh, problem here: there's a small bushfire underneath the chopper struts. Make that a big bushfire—the rotor blades are fanning the friggin' thing. The tankies fired like fuck last night and the grass must have been ignited by the gun flash ... and was still smouldering. Now it's burning! Another problem: the pilot ain't seen the fire. This could be a serious stuff-up. The Sarge is running out and yelling to French, 'Tell the fuckin' idiot to get airborne!'

French is looking down and now sees the fire, turns to the pilot and screams into the headset. The pilot turns the colour of bad shit and now we watch one of the fastest take-offs ever made by a chopper in the history of the Vietnam War—with the CQMS, white as Casper the Ghost, grabbing anything he can hang onto. This is one very bizarre sight—a bushfire in Vietnam. I say to Sarge, 'What about the fire?'

Sarge is still buckled over with laughter and says to me, 'Stuff the fire. What's it going to burn, Vietnam? Let it bloody burn.'

We still had to put it out—the only way to get our resup chopper back.

It was the nature of the Vietnam War that major units such as the Australian Task Force at Nui Dat made the province, or provinces in which they operated their own; they virtually adopted them. Unlike the World Wars, where brigades and battalions roved across wide tracts of territory—the Middle East, Europe, even the Pacific—in Vietnam one major element moved into a zone and took up residence for the whole war. So names like Bien Hoa, Ben Cat, Nha Trang, Pleiku and Phuoc Tuy became synonymous with the Allied Forces that camped there for ten years. The commanders, the troops and the logistical support came to know—for better or worse—the terrain, the towns, the villagers and the enemy. And so it followed that the ground troops revisited, again and again, places they'd been in days, weeks or months earlier. The second-tour soldiers came back after two years in Australia, and again went out to the hamlets, the mountains and the jungles of the first tour. It was depressing because nothing much changed: same bush, same mud, same rain, same smell, same Bad Guys.

So it was with some of the members of Charlie Company who were now doing their second tour of duty, when they saddled up and prepared to head west to an outpost called Xuyen Moc. The method of patrolling out here in the thickest jungle and along the wide creeks was that of fan-patrolling, box and cross-grain searches—breaking country up into digestible bites and criss-crossing grid squares—all of which involved combing one grid square at a time. A grid square on the map is a click by a click—1000 metres by 1000 metres. Across level, open terrain this would be little more than a walk in the park, but in the jungle it's a grunt's worst nightmare, especially when everyone knew that out here in the east of the province there was another hassle: the area was full of hardcore NVA and Vietcong.

Since establishing the Task Force in 1966, the Australians had come to know the villages, towns and regional centres of Phuoc Tuy extremely well. Places of major importance included Baria, (the capital) Dat Do, Long Dien and Binh Ba. The people of Binh Ba were mainly rubber-tappers, and the village was in the middle of one of the biggest plantations in the province. It was a village of particular importance to the Task Force, for not only did it straddle Route 2, the main north-south road between Phuoc Tuy and Long Khan; it also contributed significantly to the local economy and was thus a major source of tax revenue for the enemy. Binh Ba certainly had more than it's share of occupation by the VC before the Aussies kicked them out. A number of the smaller towns in Phuoc Tuy were largely pro-Australian, as was Vung Tau, a major seaport and city in its own right.

Out in the Badlands to the east was Xuyen Moc—20 kilometres east of Dat Do and 10 kilometres from the South China Sea. It comprised five or six hamlets and had a population of 1500. Xuyen Moc was the capital of the district of the same name, which covered nearly a third of the province. The town was an important regional centre from a strategic point of view, which became obvious once you learned its history. This small cluster of humanity had been almost constantly under siege; its inhabitants had known little but war and terror. In Xuyen Moc they knew a good fight when they saw one, even back in the days when the Viet Minh fought, and ultimately beat, the French. The villagers here were bled white by Vietcong tax collectors whenever they left the safety of their village, and those same VC regularly attacked the hamlet. They once penetrated the protective minefield around it, advancing as far as the surrounding moat before getting caught up in the massive barbed-wire obstacles and being driven back by a band of local Vietnamese soldiers.

In anyone's book Xuyen Moc meant grief, and certainly meant contact with a strong force of enemy. This was largely because it was a crossroads of war. Three major roads intersected near the centre of town. One of those roads, Route 23, ran from Dat Do east through Xuyen Moc into the adjoining province of Binh Tuy. Route 328 left Route 23 and headed towards the Nui May Tao Mountains, about 20 kilometres north on the border of Phuoc Tuy and Binh Tuy provinces. This was where all the aggravation came from, a major enemy stronghold which funnelled men and equipment down Phuoc Tuy's own Ho Chi Minh trail towards the larger towns. Route 329, a minor byway, left Xuyen Moc and veered into Binh Tuy—another of Charlie's supply routes.

The district comprised dense scrub and low jungle, a spider's web of ox-cart tracks and trails invisible from the air, and foot tracks laced with mines and booby-traps. Not to put too fine a point on it, the zone could break the heart of a soldier, along with quite a few other bits and pieces.

On March 17, 1971, Charlie Company's 9 Platoon, commanded by Lt Bob Lewis, hit elements of the enemy's D445 Battalion, killing one VC and wounding another. Documents on the corpse confirmed that the enemy was moving into Xuyen Moc—quite possibly on their way east to take on the Australians. Maybe even to have another go at the Task Force base.

The Goons saddled up, linked up with Anti-Tank Platoon and a section of APCs, and moved to an area north of Xuyen Moc hamlet. Boodgie, Dixie and Woody had taken a good look at the village as they passed through on foot patrol. To the diggers, this clutch of huts and knocked-together homes was the real Vietnam, the way they had imagined it—a place where war could be seen in the eyes and the faces of the people. Not just the current conflict, but war dating back to the French occupation, maybe earlier. It was a look that was hard to get a handle on—was it weariness, contempt, arrogance? No, it was resignation, acceptance. The woman who stood in the doorway of her small home made of flattened kerosene cans, quietly brushing the packed-earth floor with a palm-frond broom, had the expression of the war-wise, similar to the black-and-white World War II photos you saw of those in the Warsaw ghetto or behind the wire of a prison camp. But stride up and look straight into her face and you could read nothing in her eyes, her thin smile. Woody watched the smile expose a mouth red with betel-nut juice—Vietnamese 'chewing gum', which gradually wore away the teeth.

Boodgie grinned and winked at the children—there were no men or women of military age in the place—and they dashed over to him: 'You gip me chop, chop, gip me chigarette. I gip you green tea. You gip me chigarette now, I show you VC,' they called. Boodgie had been cautioned about giving chocolate or smokes to the Vietnamese—it was considered offensive and demeaning. The soldier handed one a Hershey Bar and the other a Marlboro.

The old woman stopped sweeping and watched the Australians from the shadow of her doorway. She wore black, blousey pyjama pants that rode up her calves, and a light grey cotton shirt. She also wore the rubber thongs that almost all Vietnamese peasants wore—the Australians called them 'Japanese riding boots'. Sometimes the sandals were fashioned from car tyres—the Aussies called those 'Ho Chi Minh sandals'. Across the dirt road a young girl quietly rocked her mamasan in a hammock, softly waving a palm frond across the older woman's face. Inside one hut Dixie could see a small fire burning, with the ubiquitous pot of green tea bubbling away. The smell here was not rotting fish and vegetables, it was more incense and woodfire mixed with pig and chicken manure. The mangiest dogs in the world trotted down the road, ignoring the chickens.

Bet those dogs wouldn't look sideways at a chook for dinner—the friggin' dog would be clobbered and tossed in the cooking pot in double-quick time.

The place was terribly poor, but there was real respect for cleanliness, the elderly and for Buddha and God—one hamlet of Xuyen Moc was entirely Catholic.

The Goons stopped for a smoke and a radio check before heading into the bush to start the operation. Another young girl stood watching the soldiers, a baby—bare bum, thumb in mouth—hitched high on her waist. She looked over her shoulder at Bob Wood.

Jesus, we think we've got a hard life, thought Woody. *This lot have known nothing but war. They're on our side, they think we're gonna win. The VC tells them otherwise, hits them for taxes and kills some of them every so often to make a bloody point. We gotta win the war or these kids are gonna be cactus.*

FULL FRONTAL

Lieutenant David Paterson hoisted his backpack up onto his enormous frame and prepared to lead his men out on patrol. The National Serviceman was commander of 8 Platoon, C Company, 3RAR. His platoon sergeant was Claude Hoppe. The platoon had been on operations since February 27, 1971; it was now March 18. The previous weeks had been spent patrolling and ambushing—heavy and frustrating work, but with no contact. Paterson and Hoppe wondered when they would see real action.

Compounding the hardship at this stage of the conflict was the fact that the Australian commitment was being wound down. There was a 'Vietnamisation' program underway whereby the war was being handed back to the South Vietnamese military—the length of the conflict, the rising body count and the protests had gradually worn down public opinion back home. US President Lyndon Johnson had succumbed in his famous 'I will not seek re-election' speech, handing over the war to the incoming Richard Nixon, who in turn pledged to end the conflict and seek 'an honourable peace' with the North.

In April, 1970, Australia decided to withdraw an Infantry battalion, leaving two battalions to do the work previously done by three. The 3rd and 4th Battalions—about 1500 men in all—now had the task of patrolling and securing Phuoc Tuy, continuing the basic duty of an Infantry unit: close with and destroy the enemy. These two battalions were now feeling the strain in an increasingly threatening environment: the enemy knew of the withdrawals and were turning up the heat. The Vietcong D445 Battalion, which had fought the Australians since their arrival, were back on their local patch and had been reinforced with elements of the 33rd NVA Regiment.

This was the situation north and north-west of Xuyen Moc when, on March 18, Paterson and his platoon stumbled upon a large enemy bunker complex. The bunker—which caused a constriction in the chest and a tightening of the sphincter muscle among the diggers—was constructed to withstand aerial bombardment and was positioned to cut up an approaching allied force. Bunkers were engineering marvels, usually interconnected by crawl tunnels, packed with overhead cover—logs and compacted dirt covered with leaves—and were almost impossible to see until an Aussie found himself standing in one, staring with a sinking feeling in his gut at the narrow slits through which a VC machine-gun or rocket propelled grenade was poking. The fire lanes were also undetectable until you crouched and looked down them. The timber reinforcing was cut from trees close by, whose stumps were later camouflaged with mud, or a fresh sapling pushed into them. From the air no-one saw the bunkers, and on the ground the first indication of one was a wall of withering fire cutting through the patrolling troops.

From a soldier's point of view, the best bunkers were the deserted ones—or those that had been flattened by a lucky strike from a B-52 pattern bombardment. Paterson had found an empty one, but the recently abandoned cooking fires indicated it hadn't long been vacated.

'About time we found something—and time we had some action,' one of 8 Platoon's soldiers, Martin Cross, said to Hoppe.

The sergeant knew in his guts his platoon was going to get action soon enough—the ingredients had been shaping up for days: tracks with fresh bootmarks, sporadic contact that other platoons had experienced in the Xuyen Moc area, and the number of bunker systems that had been found. 'It'll happen soon enough, mate,' he replied.

Paterson called an O Group, and the decision was made to split the platoon into two groups to cover more ground. Hoppe would lead one group, Paterson the other. This doubled the number of grid squares that could be searched in one day. It was an acceptable practice at the time but also a potentially dangerous one. With the chance of hitting an enemy party no more than squad size—five or six—the Aussie half-platoon method had merit. But Paterson remembered that at Canungra Jungle Training Centre he had been warned about decreasing the size of a fighting patrol to anything less than 15 men. The posted strength of a rifle platoon was one officer and 33 other ranks, including the platoon sergeant. Through attrition, transfers, sickness and lack of reinforcements, 8 Platoon was already down to 25 men. Splitting also meant that one of the groups had only one M60 machine-gun. There were three M60s to a platoon, and getting a fourth issued was almost impossible, as additional weapons were another casualty of the war since the wind-down had commenced.

On the morning of March 20, Paterson and Hoppe took their half-platoon groups out looking for the enemy, D445, and more bunkers. It was a sweltering day and Paterson bush-bashed, pushing his men until lunchtime. Resuming after the break, they had moved less than 200 metres when they found a track showing signs of ox-cart use. Then, through the silence, came the unmistakable sound of men chopping wood.

'Jeez, they're bloody confident, Skip,' Martin Cross whispered. 'Buggers are rowdier than a wood-chopping competition.'

Paterson ordered the mini-platoon to drop their packs and move into an extended line. Once they'd shaken out, he waved them further into the gloom of the thick bush. *Was it local woodcutters or the enemy?*

Paterson's scout, Alan 'Gouldy' Gould, moved to his commander's right while the machine-gun group moved to the left, the high ground. The VC were waiting less than 50 metres away in a U-shaped bunker system, and began to sight up automatic rifles, RPGs and a 12.7mm heavy machine-gun on the approaching diggers. They released the full arsenal in one deadly fusillade.

Flashback: Martin Cross—Your eardrums get blown in, then silence—then the *crack, crack* of automatic weapons like fire-crackers let off in one long string. Up above it's like Guy Fawkes night during the day, with flashes in the trees when rockets hit them. Why fire at trees? Because the detonations are throwing shrap down on us, of course. Pieces of dirt and leaves are jumping up in tiny spouts all over the place. We're on our guts, trying to get closer to the ground. The noise ... the noise ... it's deafening. Can't move forward, can't move back. Pull the rifle stock into the shoulder and fire, but what are we firing at? It's almost unreal watching the red tracers from our weapons going out and the green tracers from the enemy coming in. And the long red flashes stream-ing out from our M60 ... Patto's got blood all over his shoulder.

Paterson realised, moments before he was hit, that his half-platoon had stumbled into a bunker complex of Company size. Worse, the enemy was equipped with heavy weapons and they weren't bugging out as per normal practice, they were staying to fight. It was the D445 Vietcong unit, reinforced with regular force members of the 3/33 NVA Regiment.

Scout Alan Gould saw an M79 grenade launcher go off, heard the distinctive *dupe* it makes, then felt the blast of an incoming RPG explode nearby. He was thrown to the ground and blood began to spurt from his chest. He could taste and feel warm fluid running down his throat; he heard a curious whistling sound coming from his chest. *I've been hit in the lung.*

Paterson started crawling over to him, and shouted above the roar of fire, 'You're gonna be okay!'.

Gould's last impression was watching tracers overhead while he lay in the leaves. His section was pouring fire onto the enemy, who were still trying to close in and kill the wounded Australians. The enemy's 12.7 heavy machine-gun was cutting above Gould's head, felling small trees, and he could just see his section commander, Russ Petty, desperately trying to get to him.

One thousand metres south of Paterson's 8 Platoon, the Goons heard the contact. The men's eyes widened, and their normally red complexions from the heat of patrolling suddenly changed to grey. The soldiers knew the sounds of war, the sounds that carried Bad News—mates were copping it.

Doggy Dwyer was given the signal by his section commander to stop and prop. The Anti-Tank Platoon, which was attached to C Company, was patrolling as a full unit about 1000 metres from the Goons. The sound of gunfire had also carried to Dwyer. Everyone was getting uptight because the continuous crackle of automatic weapons and the explosions indicated a sizeable firefight. Dwyer could hear radio transmissions further back in the platoon; the sound of urgency as each commander on the battalion radio network struggled to get information. 'Who? What? What size enemy. Is any one KIA yet?'

The forward scout's senses went up a few extra notches, his eyes probed the bush to the front. *No more wandering around with my head up my arse—the bastards are right bloody here.*

The section commander, map, compass and notebook in hand, scrambled back to the scout, breathlessly panting new bearings and instructions. 'Doggy, we gotta move, fast as you can, mate. Charlie Company's in big shit and it sounds like their Sunray's been zapped.'

Dwyer lifted his rifle to cover his arc and pushed the first bushes out of the way. His mouth was dry. Quick guzzle of water. *Need a smoke. Can't have one.* Push aside another bush, eyes almost on stalks and a bucketload of sweat pouring into them. The scout had gone no more than 100 metres at a pace he felt safe with when he was faced with a huge clearing of barely waist-high grass.

'Stuff it!' he hissed.

Down on his knees, looking across 250 metres of an Infantryman's nightmare: clear ground, with the enemy somewhere to the front.

The section commander squatted behind him. 'You gotta go straight across … can't stuff around. We'll cover you with the gun. Go!'

Dwyer, Armalite up and finger checking the selector was on AUTO, walked out into the clearing. He felt his arms and legs twitching. He looked back. *Where's the friggin' gun covering me?* Move on another 20 steps, look back again. *Still no bloody gun cover. I'm going to die …*

'What the hell's going on?' The Goon Platoon sergeant was impatiently waiting for his commander, Dennis Tyson, to pass back the information. The lieutenant was holding the radio handset so hard it looked like it would break, and the skin on his face was taught.

If it'd been made of rubber it would've snapped by now, thought the sergeant, who nudged his skipper again. 'Eight's hit a bloody bunker system … are we goin' or not?'

Tyson was waiting for more information, but there were just cracks of rifle fire, interspersed with instructions from the battalion commander, who was now airborne and heading towards the contact. The sergeant stood up and swung his pack. 'We can get the bloody details on the way, let's shoot a bearing and get moving.'

The platoon commander dropped the handset. 'Right, we're moving. Get the section commanders into me and I'll brief 'em.'

Wood was pushed up front to scout, with Boodgie as a number two scout. Wood held his secateurs, ready to cut away the thick bush to his front; his hands were shaking.

Rob Betts peered down from the co-pilot's seat in his Huey Bushranger. All he could see were huge mats of thick foliage flashing beneath the gunship. He looked out his side window and saw the other Bushranger, also travelling at full clap. The light fire team had been scrambled only minutes earlier, and was now hammering in from the west towards 8 Platoon's position. The procedure would follow a set protocol: the platoon commander would speak to the light fire team, indicate where the enemy was in relation to the platoon, then smoke canisters would be thrown to mark their position. Betts wasn't to know at this stage that Dave Paterson was bleeding to death, or that the platoon had no smoke grenades left. The Bushrangers' task was to saturate the enemy with rockets and mini-gun fire, and the 23-year-old Betts readied himself to help his fellow Aussies.

Wood and Boodgie were doing more stumbling and tripping through the jungle than they were cutting a path and scouting. The two scouts were forcing the pace, watching for possible enemy, and contending with some of the thickest bush they had encountered so far. There was a need for speed, but that was impossible in this foliage, and there was a requirement to cover arcs and stop and listen. Impossible again, with sweat pouring across their faces. Both men's nerves were rubbed raw, as were those of all the Goons.

ZONE OF COURAGE

Trevor Lynch was home. Home with his mother, home safe. American surgeons had performed 30 operations on the young digger; his injuries should have killed him, but such was the nature of the Vietnam War—where men were delivered to the operating table at high speed—that he survived. The booby-trap that had exploded in front of him on the Nui Thi Vais had blown upwards from ground level and blasted across the digger, gouging and penetrating his body from just above his knees to the top of his head with dozens of small, white hot fragments. It was like he had stood in front of a steelworks furnace that had suddenly blown, leaving one- and two-inch burn marks over his upper and lower torso. Many punched deep into his body.

Lynch was home now, but the 20-year-old's world was pitch black. He had lost both his eyes.

Paterson and 8 Platoon were pinned down by a blizzard of enemy fire. 'Pinned down': an over-used, misunderstood cliché for when Vic Morrow and the men from 'Combat' are crouching behind a wall and shouting at each other to withdraw by scrambling to the rear. Pinned down in real war is flat on your guts, face in the leaves, with bullets whizzing a metre above you. Pinned down has no options: no crawl forward and certainly no scramble back, firing from the hip. Pinned down is up shit creek with no paddle. You firmly believe that this is where you, and all those with you, will die. At this stage of a contact, when soldiers are looking into the abyss, they think not only of themselves, but also their comrades. Men who fight do so not for Queen and country, politics and ideals; they fight for their mates. This has always been the true nature of combat.

David Paterson was mortally wounded; two other men, the

machine-gunner and Gould, had been hit. Things were getting worse—all the soldiers were almost out of ammunition and smoke grenades, which were desperately needed to mark their position. The spare ammo and smoke grenades were in the packs back where they'd been dropped. As their leader, Paterson knew he had to do something. Martin Cross was convinced the enemy would now advance from the bunker complex and overrun the Aussies' thin line of defence.

Paterson turned, waved his arm and called, 'Back, get back to the packs … go now, I'm covering.' He propped himself up and fired another burst from his Armalite. Cross got to his knees and worked his way backwards, crab-style, with the two men closest to him, John Melma and Ross Budden. As they reached a nearby clump of bamboo there was another sustained burst of enemy fire …

Ron Betts peered at the jungle flashing beneath him. No smoke. He now knew the firefight was intense and that the Sunray—Paterson— was down. The Bushrangers banked and wheeled over where they thought 8 Platoon was pinned down, but could see nothing. They relied on radio transmissions from Lieutenant-Colonel Peter Scott, the battalion's commanding officer who was circling over the contact area in a small Sioux helicopter in an attempt to direct the Bushranger. The CO dropped a sandbag containing smoke grenades where he thought his men were, but on the ground the men were scattered, attempting to withdraw their casualties.

Claude Hoppe, still about a click away, was anguishing over the plight of the rest of his diggers, but was ordered not to move as the Bushrangers swung in again to lay down fire.

Bob Wood and Boodgie were still scrambling flat out through the jungle. The short, lightly-built Wood adopted a technique whereby he cut away vines and the thicker growth so he could push himself forward, letting the bigger-built soldiers cope as best they could with the foliage he left behind. Sweat was streaming down his face, as much from the heat as from nerves, and his pounding heart felt like it was jumping out of his chest. He cut, took two or three paces, and fell over. He got up and resumed the cut-step-forward-fall-on-arse process. Cursing quietly, he stood up while Boodgie tried to cover him, fighting to get his composure back. Travelling quietly was impossible with the crack and snap of bushes and the collective wheezing of the platoon.

Wood reached a semi-cleared area that had obviously been recently bombed—trees leaned at crazy angles and there was evidence of gunship fire. Wood cast a quick eye around and froze, statue-still.

Flashback: Bob Wood—To the left and right are thin firing slits packed with logs and overhead cover. I'm right where I shouldn't be—in the centre of a bunker complex maybe 50 metres across. Movement! No. Breathe in and breathe out. But do not move. Will I be fired on? Is there a landmine closeby, a booby-trap strung in the trees? Wait, the scout's creed: don't just do something, stand there. Wait. Turn back to Boodgie, he's already seen them, his eyes are about to pop. Amazing how at a time like this you can actually hear your breath going in and out, in and out … and that *thump, thump,* that's your own heart …

'Get movin', Woody. It's abandoned. If there were Nogs in there you'd be bloody dead by now.' The platoon sergeant pushed through the bushes and waved the scouts on. Wood weaved and ducked through the mess of broken jungle and collapsed on the other side. He was fighting to get air back into his lungs. *This is worse than the Confidence Course at Canungra, and that's no shit.*

Boodgie caught up and patted Wood on the back. 'My turn, dickhead. Keep your bloody eyes open in future. I'll try not to walk into another Noggie bunker system.'

Wood gasped as Boodgie unsnapped his secateurs. 'Get nicked, shitlips. Wait'll you've had five minutes up front dealing with this crap.'

Boodgie took the front scout position and was soon almost up to a jog, bending and twisting through the bush and cutting in almost one continual motion. Wood followed, step by step in his mate's path. So close and tight was the vegetation—like a mineshaft—that neither man could see more than five metres to his front.

There was a crackle of radio transmission. The Bushranger was on-air. Ron Betts called for a smoke grenade from the Goons. The sergeant pulled the pin and watched the safety lever flick away, then tossed the grenade out to his front, where it hit the ground, bounced twice and began to gush purple smoke. The Bushrangers were going to take a line of flight over 7 Platoon and lay down fire in front of Paterson and his men several hundred metres away. It was not Standard Operating Procedure, but Betts figured it was one way to get rockets and gunfire in without hitting Paterson's men. There was the sound of tearing and renting as the gattling-style mini-guns opened fire from both sides of the chopper and then a whoosh of rockets. Next moment, the Iroquois clattered over like a barracuda barrelling in for the kill. Shell casings from the mini-guns rained down on the Goons.

Betts felt the chopper lurch left as his pilot banked across the fire zone. The team had laid down fire and now decided to make a smoke grenade drop so the men on the ground could toss more smoke. The Bushranger slowed to a hover over where Betts thought the men were and the door gunner prepared to drop the sandbag of grenades. The co-pilot looked down. Something was wrong: there were green tracers coming straight up at the gunship. *Enemy fire!* They had come in on the wrong fire line and were directly over the enemy bunker complex. Twenty enemy rounds ripped into the Bushranger. Betts jerked and slumped forward, blood pouring out from under his helmet.

'What do you mean, *bloody leaving,* they only just got here!' The Goon sergeant stood and tried to look up beyond the trees for the Bushranger gunships. The radio spat and crackled. 'Bushranger taken heavy ground fire … we've got one WIA.'

Jacko, the Goons' radio man, was still listening to the transmission. 'Serious stuff. He's not good and they're pulling out.'

The sergeant squatted. 'Jesus, why? Only one's been hit. Couldn't they stay and help?'

'They're a team, mate,' said Tyson. 'They cover each other in and out: one in, all in—one out, all out.'

Scouting across the clearing, Doggy Dwyer looked up for a moment at the Bushranger gunships to his front and east. One chopper banked and then flattened out with streams of tracer pouring ahead of it. *Mini-guns.* The helicopter banked and wobbled and turned to the west, suddenly obscured by trees.

Dwyer was still feeling like the loneliest man in the world. He could hear himself panting; his mouth was as dry as a salt pan. *Look behind. Jesus, still no-one following.* They were going to wait and see if he got shot. In his mind's eye he could see the VC lining him up, taking a bead: the sudden zap as the bullet drove a neat hole in his head and blew out the other side … *Twenty metres left, still alive, 10 more … five.* The last five paces were a half-stagger and stumble as the scout crashed down near the base of the trees. He crawled forward and checked his immediate front.

*All still. Check my fire position. Use the shadows, stay out of sunlight—
Canungra JTC: run, down, crawl, observe, aim, fire.*

Silence in here, apart from the crackle of gunfire from 8 Platoon's
position. Dwyer worked his way back to the clearing in a half
crouch and held his arm up, thumb extended. *All clear, I'm still here,
get over here, you bloody slugs.* His section commander appeared in the
distance with the M60 gunner to his right, then two more bobbing
Aussie bush hats. Dwyer fumbled for a cigarette. *Stuff security, gotta
have a smoke.*

The members of 8 Platoon were fighting for their lives. The wall
of fire had become sporadic and the platoon popped its last
smoke grenade to assist an ammunition drop. The moment the
coloured smoke began to filter upwards, another smoke grenade
popped and sent the same colour upwards—inside the enemy
perimeter. Martin Cross's heart sank. *They've used the same coloured
smoke. Cunning bastards, they were waiting for that.*

With John Melma and Ross Budden, Cross crawled through
clumps of bamboo, trying to find where they had dropped their
packs. *Got to get more ammo.* The three squatted and peered back
at the contact area at the moment the Bushrangers came in. There
was a long burst of what sounded like AK-47 fire. The gunships
swept over the position and droned away to the southwest.

Some time later, section commander Russ Petty appeared
through the thick bush with two other men. 'Can't get to Patto—
fire's still too heavy.'

The men spread out and waited. There was movement to their
front and instinctively all the soldiers knew it was enemy. Petty
hissed, 'Don't fire yet … hold it back.'

Cross suddenly felt like this was it. He was certain he was living his last moments. He had two hand grenades left. 'What we
gonna do if they come and have a go?'

Petty looked at Melma and Budden. 'We got about 30 rounds left, you reckon? Wait until they're on top of us then give 'em the bloody lot … '

Now silence. Cross scanned the front and glanced back over his rear shoulder. More movement behind. He spun around and waited for the first figures to appear. *They look like bloody Nogs, Jesus.* Then he saw grins and thumbs-up as Lieutenant Peter Abigail and his Pioneer Platoon arrived. *Just like the movies, the Cavalry turns up just as the good guys are about to be creamed.*

TOUGH BREAKS

You walk through the jungle where there has just been a firefight. The event has passed but there is a resonance. Look at the men. You try to read the faces; you can't. You try and catch snippets of conversation, words that will somehow give a glimpse of what just happened. Nobody says a word about it; that will come later, in short exchanges—soldiers' shorthand—probably in the Company boozer. For now, just one thing is important: got to make a brew and have a smoke. Make that two, three smokes.

Soldiers are squatting near each other, some are lying or sitting, all eyes are to the front—looking *out there*. That's where they were. Look around you at the bunkers, now blown up or crushed by the weight of the Centurion tanks. *That's where they were, in there, in those bloody holes in the ground they're so fond of.* Sip a hot brew; time to be thankful. *Thanks, God, for sparing me. Thanks blokes for getting here, thanks tankies for crushing their bunkers.* You also thank those marvellous men in the Bushrangers. You would like to, but know you can't thank the pilot, now lying dead at the Vampire Hospital—shot down in the air directly above where you're now sipping coffee.

Thanks, too, for the fact that we're not all dead, like the officer lying on the seat in the back of the armoured carrier. Lt David Paterson, KIA, March 20, 1971. As you walk past the APC you have to look; you don't want to, but you have to. Patto, the gentle giant with boots so big they're handmade; Patto the Nasho, liked by all. Patto now lying on the seat of the carrier. He still has a few blades of grass in his hand, grass he must have clutched as he died. *Maybe in a minute he'll get up and walk out and ask for a brew. Hell, why would they make such a huge man an Infantry commander? Men that big don't belong in the jungle, the jungle's for shorter people—people you don't see so easy.*

'Fuck this dirty bloody war!' Butch was throwing another of his memorable wobblies. 'Okay, that's it. Bloody Charlie's no friend of mine. Charlie's killed one of my mates, so from here on out every Charlie's cactus.'

The dustoff arrived to take the dead and wounded. Butch put his hand up when asked to help carry Paterson to the chopper. But the Goon medic, Peter Forbes, held his hand up before the task was under way. 'You're not sending Patto out with the wounded, Sarge—it's the golden rule: dead and wounded in separate choppers.'

The Goon sergeant realised he'd made a mistake. 'We can't wait all day for another dustoff, Forbesy.'

The medic was adamant. 'The rule is, the wounded never travel with the dead. I don't give a toss how you do it, Sarge, but the wounded aren't travelling with their dead skipper.' Forbes wheeled and walked away.

Later that day a second dustoff came in. Paterson was loaded on to the Iroquois with as much gentleness as the Goons could muster. You couldn't help but notice the one huge boot that stuck out from the poncho liner wrapped around the body. There was a rubber band around it to stop the detached sole flapping. He would have walked many clicks with that rubber band around his boot—and it would have been a real bastard, snagging on every vine he stepped over. The Army just didn't have spare boots that size to fly in on a resupply.

***

Doggy Dwyer was still hyperventilating when his section commander and the machine-gunner, Jim Merrin, reached him at the edge of the clearing.

The section commander grinned at his scout. 'Well done, Doggy, didn't think you'd make it for a while.'

Dwyer gasped for breath. 'Make it? Bloody make it? I coulda

got a round in the melon walking across that ...'

'What are you so pissed off about? We had to send someone out to draw fire—there's Nogs out here, don't you know?' The section commander winked and grinned, moving aside as Merrin, almost buried under belts of ammunition, pushed into the trees. He paused a moment to look at the scout whose face had turned from white back to red in the space of a few minutes. 'Heck, Doggy, thought we'd lose you there for a minute. What sort of dickhead walks across a clearing in Nog country? For Pete's sake!'

Merrin chuckled while Dwyer slumped next to a tree and sulked.

The second scout, Les McNicholl, was brought up to take the lead. He smiled at his fellow scout. 'Hey Doggy, you look like dry dog shit. You okay, mate?'

Dwyer dropped back into the section and the men took up fire positions as the rest of the platoon crossed the clearing.

There was a certainty when death was there, right alongside you. It was there today. Never felt it before, the absolute and total vulnerability of being killed, and able to do nothing about it. Like sitting behind the wheel of a car heading off a cliff.

After 15 minutes working towards the 8 Platoon position, Dwyer was regaining his sense of humour and plotting his payback.

Colin Cogswell, the youngest man in 5th Battalion, was not old enough to vote, hardly old enough to drink, and—after he got home—still could not comprehend what had happened in his few months in Vietnam. He had landed in Vietnam, seen action, seen Australians die. He had tried to absorb the whys and wherefores of the war—its complexities, its people, the place—and had been almost blown to pieces. And now the war had finished for him ... and he was still only 19. At 2 Camp Hospital undergoing treatment for the mine blast injuries, Cogswell's head was still spinning.

Flashback: Colin Cogswell—Everything happened so fast in Vietnam. One minute you were in the tent at Nui Dat, the next aboard a Huey beating out to a place where both sides were hell bent on killing each other. When you were wounded, it was up and out of the jungle with a windblast in your face, under the knife, out of the operating theatre, in a Hercules and back in Australia, where you sat in a pub and watched on black-and-white TV the war you had just left. How bloody weird was that?

You couldn't catch your breath over there. You couldn't grieve for the dead like they did in the World Wars. No standing over a grave—if your mate was dead, he was in a body bag, in a Huey and bloody gone before you could say goodbye or take a final look. Vietnam was speed and expediency—*hurry up and wait.*

Cogswell was a war hero. He received the Military Medal on the recommendation of his Company Commander, Bruce McQualter—later killed in the Long Hais mine blast—for his coolness and bravery during action in the Nui Thi Vais on Operation Canberra in October 1967.

But the young digger felt his youth had been burned out of him. While other Australians his age were chasing girls, driving hot cars, surfing and generally being cool, Cogswell was contending with pain and the isolation of having left his mates behind. His peers looked at this odd young man and wondered what planet he had been living on, what he had done that had caused so much pain in a person of such tender years?

He arrived in Adelaide in a propeller-driven Viscount and was admitted to Repatriation Hospital at Daw Park. His wounds were dressed and he was given the all-clear to get back to soldiering, but he was a shadow of the soldier who went to war: his weight had dropped, and his injuries and the post-traumatic stress had sapped his energy.

Cogswell still had three years of service left. Transferred back to active duty in Sydney, he bought a 1964 EH Holden. He tried to get on with life back at 5RAR, but couldn't settle. He hit the booze, was downgraded medically, and had to leave the Infantry. He was posted to the Engineers.

Life months after Vietnam was on a slide for Cogswell. There was another operation on his knee to remove more shrapnel, and then he went through another shocking and life-changing experience: he was a passenger in an Army truck that collided head-on with another one. The ex-forward scout suffered multiple fractures to his pelvis and lower back, and was in hospital for three months. Laying prostrate, and again in debilitating pain, the 19-year-old war hero figured that this time his soldiering days were over.

SHAPE SHINE SHADOW

The Infantry has been around forever, has fought in every kind of uprising and conflict since men first took up powder and ball and marched into walls of fire like they were on a parade-ground rather than a battleground. When men dropped screaming to the ground beside them, they too screamed, to galvanise each other, and simply marched onward. They have bled and died in every corner of the Earth and on the most remote and isolated battlefields imaginable. The Australian Infantryman has fought in many wars all over the world—and the battlefields have rarely been chosen by us.

In all battles, as one line of Infantry falls in the firestorm of fighting, another replaces it. Such is and always has been the nature of warfare. The Australian Infantryman has staggered across 'No Man's Land' in France, grasped for a handhold on a rocky outcrop they called 'the Sphinx' at Gallipoli, dug holes in the shattered earth like rats at Tobruk, and struggled up the jungle track at Kokoda. It was always the Infantryman who went forward to locate the enemy, then call in the artillery, tanks and air support. The commanders and scientists of war figured out long ago that, despite all the aircraft, bombs and artillery in their arsenal, to take and hold ground you must have Infantry.

The Infantryman's weapon has evolved from the blunderbuss and musket to the cartridge rifle, which in turn became the single-shot Winchester, and on to the semi-automatic rifle and the fully automatic machine-gun that can mow down with enfilade fire an entire line of men. Weapons are all about fire rates and firepower. In Vietnam they ranged from the basic unit from previous wars, the 9mm sub-machine gun, up to the general purpose machine-gun, the portable, gas-operated, belt-fed M60, which had a cyclic rate of 550 rounds per minute. Infantry also had shoulder-fired weapons: World War II bazookas, Vietnam's M72 light anti-tank weapons, and the shotgun-style M79 40mm grenade launcher.

Then there were the indirect weapons, expensive and lethal—mortar and field artillery pieces, tanks and gunships. Look to the sky: the fighter with machine-guns, napalm and B-52 strikes—mega-death, 500 to 1000 pounds of explosive, which sometimes bored into the ground before exploding, causing localised earthquakes. All this, and *still* the enemy in the jungle remained undefeated. It all came back to a man with a rifle, who had to go and find the Bad Guys before all this ordnance could be brought to bear.

A thousand feet above the jungle, seated on the deck of the Huey with his legs folded beneath him and with cool air on his face, Doggy Dwyer briefly stopped thinking about bombs and bullets. He sat there admiring the beauty of South Vietnam. It had in the last few years been burned and bombed a bit, for sure, but it was still a country of tropical Asian serenity: swaying palms, plantations of banana and pepper, and elegant stands of commercial rubber. Then there was the natural exuberance and magnificence of the thick green, wet jungle. *From up here, how many shades of green can you count?*

Look out the portside door to the west—quilts of wet rice padis, sunlight flashing over them as the chopper bobbed and rocked. Further west, the rising Nui Thi Vais, a washed-out grey from here but quiet, permanent and menacing. Look over the north-east—the rising, dense jungle around the May Tao Mountains. The enemy was thick in there, too, Dwyer had been told; but from here it was unexplored territory, like you read about in schoolboy adventure books.

The slicks carrying the Infantry began to descend. Men shuffled on the floor of the aircraft, checked packs, made sure their hats were shoved inside their shirts, and fidgeted with a map in the pocket, a grenade on the belt and bandoliers of ammunition.

Stupid, unnecessary—if you haven't got it with you now, mate, too late.

There was a clearing ahead, near a tiny hamlet called Thua Tich. There were only the remains of the village on Route 328; it had long ago been rocketed by the VC and defoliated by the Americans. The VC were back, and the Australians were launching another operation to recapture territory lost years before. That was Vietnam: take it one day, lose it the next; take it the following week, lose it the month after. With no frontline, the conflict was like a game of billiards, with combatants cannoning off each other, scattering and re-gathering to have another go.

Dwyer and his section were off and running under the chopper downwash. *Hit the deck, don't run too far, look left and right. 'Soon as the choppers piss off, head for the low bush and go into a defensive position.*

The Anti-Tank Platoon was to be part of the main force establishing a fire support base (FSB)—the Vietnam phenomenon where the allies built their own version of a fortified village, bristling with wire and weaponry. Any soldier involved in combat operations in Vietnam knew what a FSB was: days of back-breaking work in the sun; long nights with no sleep; a place where mortars and rockets could come in night or day. Fire bases were clouds of dust in the Dry, lakes of mud in the Wet. The purpose was to establish a forward area where the artillery could be flown in and bedded down to offer fire support to the Infantry, out on search and destroy missions.

Constructing a FSB involved filling a thousand sandbags, laying three-strand 'cattle fences', then rolling out concertina wire—three-tier-high barbed-wire hoops. Fire bases also meant digging in—digging in to dirt as hard as concrete, or shovelling slop out of a one-man weapon pit (Vietnam's version of the foxhole) that became a brown-water bathtub in the monsoon. During the day, the men building the base had a miserable choice: patrol and ambush in the jungle around the base, or dig weapon pits and fill sandbags. The choice was redundant—the Infantryman did both.

This construction had to be done super-fast—Charlie knew what was going on, what those 105 artillery pieces were for, and he tried his damnedest to neutralise them. Ground assault, human wave-style, was unusual but not unheard of against a FSB. The NVA had hit two bases, Coral and Balmoral, in 1968; and Coral was nearly overrun. That was a few clicks north in Long Khan province, and it possibly involved elements of the 33rd NVA Regiment—the same hardcore soldiers believed to be in the vicinity of 3rd Battalion, now building FSB Ziggie. Fire bases were named after senior officers' wives, girlfriends or daughters. No digger ever had his wife's name given to a FSB. Who the hell would want their girl's name given to one of these outposts of misery?

On the ground now, the Infantry started doing what Infantrymen have done in all modern wars—dig. Get below ground, pack sandbags around the edge of the weapon pit, check or cut fire lanes, make out range cards and stake the M60s on fixed arcs. The grunt did all this on auto-pilot. Problem on day one: someone had forgotten to get the sandbags flown in.

'Don't worry about it. We're going out on ambush.' Dwyer's section commander gave a warning order, and an hour before last light, Dwyer took the lead as his section moved out from the perimeter into the trees. In the first five-minute break, the scout was watching Jim Merrin smoke. Payback time. Like most Infantry soldiers, Dwyer and Merrin had paired off in the war—whispered to each other quietly on gun sentry, made each other brews, shared a few personal secrets, had a few blues in the bush, but nothing serious. There was, however, a noticeable difference between them: Dwyer was a smart-arse, fast with a practical joke. The powerfully-built Merrin was quiet, sometimes introverted, and couldn't see a joke coming even when it had his name on it.

This was one of the reasons Merrin became a member of the Phantom Club. Being spotted leaving the latrine with a *Phantom* comic in his hand led, several weeks later, to the arrival of a large envelope addressed to 'Private James Merrin of the 3rd Battalion'. Inside was the latest *Phantom* comic, a club membership card and a black-and-white photo of the masked hero, personally signed by 'The Ghost Who Walks'. Merrin didn't explode immediately, but went on a slow burn, swearing vengeance against whoever had nominated him. Later, Big Jim saw the humour, and even agreed to wear his personal plastic Phantom Skull ring—although he could only jam it onto the first knuckle on his little finger. Someone put Vegemite on the ring, so if Merrin punched you, it left the legendary skull mark.

During the first weeks in the bush, platoon members would also seek advice from Merrin on how Mr Walker would behave in the bush—'Do you reckon he'd come out of his skull cave while it's pissin' down like this, Jim?'

'No way. Old jungle saying: Man Who Goes Out In Rain Is Wettex.'

'You reckon the Phantom would carry an M16, Jim?'

'No way, Ghost Who Walks wears pistols, has Guran to carry M60.'

Dwyer sat down next to his mate. 'Jim, had a bloody horrible nightmare last night, mate. We were on patrol in scrub just like this and you got shot by a Noggie as you were stepping over a log.'

The big gunner nearly swallowed his cigarette. 'That's not fuckin' funny, Doggy.'

'Naw, mate, was only a dream, just bullshit. And you only got hit in the shoulder … but hell, it was clear.'

The patrol moved off with Merrin shooting looks at Dwyer every time the scout stopped for a break. Dwyer started chuckling to himself. With every log the patrol came to—and there were thousands—Merrin detoured almost all the way around it, squinting nervously into the trees. By the time the gunner had almost exhausted himself on the hundredth log, Dwyer and half the section were fighting back tears of laughter. The last thing Dwyer remembered before settling into the night ambush was the gunner threatening to decapitate him with a machete when he was asleep.

A day later, the section commander had salt instead of sugar in his brew, and two other diggers who had made smart remarks about Dwyer's deadly clearing crossing found centipedes in their sleeping silks. Payback completed.

Charlie Company and the Goon Platoon had been airlifted from near Xuyen Moc to an area they were to patrol in preparation for the next major operation. In the last week of March, the Goons reached the banks of the Song Rai River, the largest watercourse in Phuoc Tuy. The men stopped, not because they had reached a river—a natural obstacle that had to be crossed tactically anyway—but because of the surreal picture that now greeted them. Other units had previously patrolled along this riverbank on the Thua Tic side and named the area the 'Gobi Desert'. You couldn't miss it from the air, and at ground level it was shocking—like stumbling into another country.

The area around this once well-populated village used to be rich farmland. Now, with Thua Tic destroyed and the vegetation defoliated, there was nothing but stark, barren land: few trees, no leaves, and ground that had turned pale brown and grey. This was the result of massive defoliation, not bulldozing. The defoliant, a powerful poison sprayed from the air, settled on and killed all vegetation, creating a moonscape—like the soldiers had moved from jungle fighting to desert warfare. On the other side of the river was thick jungle, as though the Song Rai formed a natural border between the lush jungle vegetation and an arid zone.

The men took a short halt, taking up fire positions as best they could in this desolate landscape. Soon, several men scrambled down to fill their water bottles under the cover of machine-guns. Woody and Dixie began to chatter while they filled their canteens.

The Goon sergeant hissed at his men. 'Shut the fuck up. Every Nog within a thousand yards'll hear you. Sound carries along water, you bloody idiots.'

Just as the sergeant finished giving his men a spray, he received a gentle nudge from Jacko, the signaller. Jacko's face was as white as a sheet. Pointing across the river, he said, 'Sarge, I just saw a Nog watching me from over there.'

The sergeant kneeled and pulled up his rifle, one eye on the men on the riverbank, the other on the trees. *Look through the trees, not at them. Look for movement, shape, shine, shadow, surface, silhouette and spacing.*

Nothing.

'Musta been a monkey.' The sergeant clicked his fingers and motioned the men up and away from the river. One last look back. Nothing, only the stillness of the jungle and an unsettling feeling. A grunt knows when something's wrong; the antennae twitch. There's an intuition about being watched, when someone's surely got their sights on you, taking a bead on your skull. You can feel it. Like now …

The Goons moved on.

Next day, April Fool's Day, a platoon from 2nd Battalion's A Company—on this joint operation with 3rd Battalion—

reached the same location on the river, but on the jungle side. They discovered that the 'monkey' that Jacko had seen the day before became five 'monkeys', then a company-sized enemy bunker system. Obviously, the VC had not fired on the Goons for fear of having the bunker system discovered and destroyed. The enemy wrongly assumed that the Goon Platoon was a patrol working along the cleared side of the river, and were best left alone. In minutes the platoon that bumped the bunker system was hit from three sides with automatic fire and RPGs. Had the enemy fired on the Goons in the open the day before, the results would have been catastrophic.

Bushrangers took to the air and raced to the Song Rai River, where another 2RAR/NZ(ANZAC) platoon moved up to support the one already pinned down and taking casualties. Tanks rolled in from Highway 328. Three Battalion's CO, Lieutenant-Colonel Scott, had tried to drop additional smoke grenades; the enemy had thrown the same coloured smoke to cause confusion in the air. The first dustoff chopper on the scene went to the wrong smoke, and its door gunner was killed by a burst of enemy fire.

The firefight quickly developed into a major battle: the enemy brought mortar fire down on the Australians, who beat a withdrawal from the bunker system back towards the river. The enemy quickly adopted a 'hug the belt' strategy, staying close to the diggers, knowing they couldn't risk taking more casualties by calling down hellfire and brimstone from the artillery and Bushrangers.

Looking down at the belting the men on the ground were getting, Colonel Scott was filled with frustration and anger. Suddenly a burst of automatic fire raked across the machine. Scott yelled to his pilot on the intercom, 'We're over the enemy! Get the hell out!' One round slammed up between the seats of the two men, and the aircraft jerked suddenly, the oil pressure gauge plunged. The pilot carried out an emergency drill, successfully landing on the eastern bank of the Song Rai. The men scrambled from the machine and ran, fearing an explosion. They travelled approximately 200 metres before meeting up with the Centurion tanks.

The Goons wheeled and began to beat a path back towards the action. Again, as with C Company's 8 Platoon, the Goons could hear the firefight erupt and intensify, saw the Bushrangers fly in for their strike and the dustoff come beating in from the south-west. Jacko shook his head. 'Told you that was a Nog lookin' at us yesterday.'

The sergeant was annoyed, and said sharply, 'Somebody's always seeing something, aren't they Jacko? For Christ's sake, we had a good look and saw bugger-all. We can count ourselves lucky we thought it was a monkey—if we'd have tried to cross the river to check it out yesterday, not one of us would be alive today.'

The next day, the Goons moved into the bunker system to mop up. It was the same story: the enemy had fled, leaving blood and bandages scattered around 32 individual enemy bunkers spread over an area 350 by 200 metres. Documents showed it was home to the D445 VC Battalion, who had a heavy weapon company and NVA reinforcements. These were soldiers ready to fight, hold ground, and take on almost any 'invader'.

Flashback: Goon Sergeant—I've been here before. Second tour, and nothing changes. The only changes have been in my head. I had to come back to Vietnam because I felt I hadn't finished the job first time. I'm not going to finish it this time, either. Charlie knows we're going home and he'll still be here. He's going to finish *his* job. The most important thing now is to get us all home alive. That's my mission now. This war's knackered, and we certainly aren't going home as conquering heroes. I just have to get my blokes and myself out of here with our balls intact. After all who wants to be remembered as *the last Australian killed in Vietnam?*

FIRE BASE BLUES

For Ted Harrison, sleep had become a strange landscape. He sat bolt upright in bed, covered in sweat, his chest so tight he thought an elephant was kneeling on it. In bed at night, he would toss and turn and *listen*. It wasn't the loud, consistent sounds—traffic, aircraft, dogs barking down the street—it was the small sounds, like the distant squeak of a gate or the scratching of an insect on the window.

Alice Harrison still fussed over her son. She did everything he didn't want her to do, smothering the veteran with kindness that was becoming increasingly hard for Ted to take. She sometimes held him close.

I'm still her little boy. He could feel the wetness of her tears on his cheek. She didn't understand. How could she? Even Ted didn't know what was raging in his head. He crept away to the isolation he was craving—to the far reaches of the back garden, anywhere he could be alone and where his mother couldn't see him break down and sob.

At night it was back to his room, *listening*. He lay awake, rocking with the pain in his stomach until he collapsed with exhaustion. Weeks after his return home, and still that nightmare came back every night. In the morning, the sheets were pulled all over his bed and the details of the nightmare had completely gone. Before sleeping the next night, he would try again to capture the visions. They wouldn't come.

Harrison went out to the RSL, where his age was questioned, and into the pubs to see his mates—'Ted, sorry I didn't come to see you, but it's great to have you back.' He felt like an attraction at the zoo when Alice took him out to do the rounds of the relatives. The normality of the outside world seemed crazy to him. While everybody was whingeing about life—the price of beer, the scarcity of good tradesmen and the useless politicians— the veteran kept automatically reaching for his rifle before he walked outside. *No rifle, can't go outside yet.*

And then there was the guilt that he was back in Sydney while his mates were still *over there*. Over there, where he'd learned to listen so intently at night. His hearing became so acute, he thought he could hear a leaf fall a hundred metres away.

The word was that in another life, Trahn Tihn was a Warrant Officer (WO) in the North Vietnamese Army. In this life he was a Bushman Scout in the Australian Army. Tihn was attached to 2nd Battalion and had been posted to the Anti-Tank/Trackers unit. As far as we knew, no-one had ever verified the story about him being former NVA, but it sounded good, and over the years the Bushmen Scouts had come to thrive on myth and past feats with their old mates, the Vietcong.

The scouts were a problem for the diggers: most of them were former enemy, and they looked and acted like Vietnamese soldiers—not like members of the Army of the Republic of Vietnam (ARVN), who were on our side, but like the VC. When you looked at a Bushman Scout in the jungle you'd swear you were looking at a Nog. Whose side was someone like Tihn *really* on? If they were no longer loyal to their old NVA mates, how could they be trusted to be loyal to us? The scouts spent their time in Nui Dat or with the diggers in the bush—which was a rarity, because the Australians had a policy of not employing Vietnamese civilians or soldiers, and certainly not allowing them near or into the Task Force precincts. Obviously, Australian command considered the Bushman Scout a valuable asset.

Tihn used to while away his hours in his hammock when back at Nui Dat or on a FSB, singing and humming Vietnamese love ballads until a soldier became so pissed off with the whine, he tossed a snake into the hammock. Tihn shot into the air and gave the ballads a break, but he could count himself lucky: other Bushman Scouts had real reason to panic when they walked back to the tent at night in Nui Dat and saw an inebriated digger, rifle at the shoulder, drawing a bead on them.

One day Johnno was walking back from a weapon pit on a FSB with a distressed look on his face, clutching his stomach. 'Jesus, I won't do that again. I just tried some of Tihn's Noggie rations—curried fish heads and rice. Had to drink half a bloody jerry-can to wash the stuff down.'

Matusch and the other soldiers sitting in the shade sympathised with Johnno, who was warming to his subject and looking at Tihn. Tihn was serenading again.

'Fish heads and rice, ain't that the good stuff, Tihn? Bloody idiot's got no idea what we're talking about, have ya, Tihn? Go back to singing about your Noggy girlfriend, you make me sick with your lovesick bullshit.' Tihn looked over and gave the Australians a huge smile and a thumbs-up. Former NVA or not, you had to like him.

Second Battalion's A Company had taken a mauling in the Song Rai ambush; Matusch's platoon was put on a warning order about an operation under way to hunt down the enemy who had fled the bunker. Matusch was told in the Orders Group he would be among those who would pick up the slack for A Company until they could get reinforcements. It struck Matusch that the unit he was travelling with was packing some heavyweight additional personnel: Assault Pioneers with mine-detecting equipment, a mortar platoon forward controller, an artillery forward controller and, remarkably, a forward air controller doing ground duty who could call in air strikes. His platoon commander was the reliable and competent Lieutenant John Alcock, who indicated the direction and distance they would head out from the FSB.

The briefing gave all the necessary information, but was light on destination and possible enemy strength.

There were 28 men in the patrol. Their ten-day mission was to head north towards Long Khan, out of range of Australian guns and within range of a Thai Army artillery unit. This caused a few nerves: no-one had had any experience calling in artillery from anyone but Aussie, Kiwi or American guns.

It was 0700 hours when the platoon moved to a point outside the perimeter wire on the road. The Hueys came floating in, kicked up their usual dust storm, and were soon up and banking north. Matusch looked down to see one of Phuoc Tuy's legendary landmarks—the White Lady, a statue of the Madonna several storeys high that, through some miraculous intervention, was still standing in a landscape bombed into the Stone Age. As the slicks touched down, the men jumped into a grassy clearing and were soon in the jungle. Matusch was just working up a sweat when he got a sign from the man in front—a finger drawn across the throat. Moments later he was looking down at the skeletal remains of a NVA soldier. He felt his scalp prickle. *All this fire-power and secrecy—we're going into something big.*

Doggy Dwyer and the Anti-Tank Platoon were filling sandbags at FSB Ziggie when the Goons arrived and heard the news that they would be laying wire around the base.

'Great, just bloody great!' Wood, Dixie and Butch spoke as one. 'Stuff it, Sarge can't we go back out into the weeds?'

'What the bloody hell do we know about wiring?'

'One whole day of lessons back at Murray Bridge Range was all we had on real defence, wasn't it?'

The sergeant's mind was racing—*How the hell do we prevent a full-blown mutiny? Fletcher Christian's mob on the 'Bounty' would have nothing on this lot if they went off. Fuckin' wiring? I did shed-loads of it on my last tour with 5RAR. Why the bloody hell don't they just get those blokes to do it and let us get back to what we do? Soldiers hate putting up wire; we see it in the same way a dog sees a door—it's just an obstacle that we're permanently on the wrong side of.*

God was listening that day, for at that very moment he placed a RAEME armoured personnel carrier directly in the sergeant's line of sight. Known as the 'White Winged Warrior', it differed from the usual APC in that it had a crane on top and was painted white down its sides. The sergeant knew it wasn't busy carrying personnel: it was a recovery and repair vehicle crewed by specialised RAEME mechanics. They carried all sorts of spare parts and tools and would go anywhere when called upon to assist their mates in the tanks and APCs.

Perhaps today they can assist us?

Wood and Boodgie stood beside the machine and watched their sergeant duck inside with a 'Hang about for a minute.'

'You blokes own this thing?'

'Yeah, why, you wanna lift somewhere?'

'No, but I've got a bit of a problem. The CO's given us just four days to put wire around this joint, and I don't reckon we can do it.'

'Typical, Sarge, bloody officers want everything done yesterday.'

'Yeah, but I'm wondering if they aren't telling us everything— could be the 274 Regiment is four days from here and we're going to make a stand in this place … you know, sort of like Balmoral or Coral, if you know what I mean. Could be we're going to need the wire up faster than the CO's letting on.'

There was a moment's silence. 'Sarge, you could be right. What can we do to help?'

'Lend us the carrier.'

'Can you drive?'

'Shit, mate, I was a plant operator before I came over here.'

By mid-afternoon, with the sergeant at the controls, two men on the top of the machine, two inside and two on the lowered back ramp, the platoon had laid down the first rolls of concertina wire around the entire perimeter. The men inside passed steel star pickets through the hatch to the men up top, who lined them up and hammered them in with dollies while the blokes on the ramp strung the wire. It was a production line effort that Henry Ford would have been proud of

Later in the day, Battalion CO Scott encountered the Goons doing their mobile fencing.

'Where did you get the APC from, Sergeant?' The CO's moustache twitched with disapproval.

'Borrowed it from the RAEME boys. They weren't using it at the time, sir. It's been great for getting the vegetation down.'

Colonel Scott looked at the machine, then rolled his eyes, 'Carry on, but don't flatten too much vegetation. We need it for cover as much as the enemy does, you know.'

The sergeant stopped sweating, got back into the seat and kicked the engine over again.

Inside the firebase, Doggy Dwyer was preparing to dig his personal weapon pit. About 50 metres to his rear, the Battalion HQ group had used the Assault Pioneers to dig bunkers for the commanders. That was the way the war went—the grunts have to dig their own and do a thousand other jobs, the officers are always 'busy' and get some other poor bastard to do it for them.

Fearing that the enemy might mortar the position that first night, everyone urgently wanted to get below ground level before dark. Dwyer noticed the Goons trundle by in 'their' APC. They all wore the kind of grin you'd see on a young bloke back home when he'd just taken delivery of his first BSA motorcycle.

Bloody brilliant idea, using a machine to do it. Good grunt initiative.
About half an hour later, two officers walked along inspecting
the wire. Wouldn't you know it, they weren't happy, so they told
the anti-tank section commander to move the wire. The commander simply shrugged, shook his head and walked over to the
resting Dwyer and his mates.

'They want the wire to our front moved out 20 feet. And you
guessed it—we gotta do it.'

The only thing worse than putting up barbed wire is taking it
down, and taking it down after half an hour to move it 20 feet
really is an insult. The diggers were fit to be tied: there was more
cursing in that hour than at any other time since Dwyer had
arrived in Vietnam. Dwyer got back from the wire covered in
scratches. He'd got his weapon pit down more than a foot when
the two officers came over again. After a quick consultation: 'The
pits will have to be moved out another 20 feet as well.'

The air turned blue. The soldiers filled in the weapon pits
they'd already dug to a reasonable depth and struggled in the
fast-fading light to dig new ones. The section commander trotted
around with a handful of empty sandbags. 'We're not going to do
it in time. Take these bags, fill two and put one each side of your
head if any shit comes in later tonight.'

Dwyer recognised the tip to stay alive from a bloke who was on
his second tour of duty, but couldn't resist the urge to have a go.
'Any sand with these bags? What do we use to fill 'em with?'
The scout got 'the look' from his section commander and started
scraping up whatever dirt he could.

Flashback: Doggy Dwyer—Seven and a wakey. The war's over in
seven and a wake-up. I'm going home. My time in the Army is finished and I'll be flying away from Ziggie, back to the Dat and then
onto Saigon and home. They asked me long ago why I signed up

for three years. I said I'd see if I liked it before I signed up for another three. No-one in their right mind could say they liked Vietnam ... but something's happened to me here. Challenge? Fulfilment? Anger and bitterness? I'm not sure what it is ...

YIPPEE MATES

The Goons humped their way through another all-day patrol, crossed narrow creeks, struggled up muddy inclines, and now sat smoking and munching biscuits in the rain. Upon arrival in Vietnam, many diggers went to the trouble of pulling out plastic hootchies to wrap around their shoulders and over their head to keep the water out. No hope. By the third month in the jungle, during monsoon, you just sat there and got pelted, hand cupped around a cigarette. You couldn't talk because the rain was bulleting so hard on the canopy. Sit and stare ahead, suck on the smoke and think about the new car, the times when you could relax, really relax, back home. *Down at the pub; now we can go to the RSL. Go and sit on the jetty again and fish. Like we did years ago, it seems. And sex, lots of sex you don't have to pay for.*

Jacko sat quietly with the handset glued to his ear. He took his job seriously: he once told the Sarge to piss off after he'd grabbed the handset and barked orders into it. 'I'm not your bloody caddy on the golf course, Sarge. Tell me and I'll do the relaying—it's my bloody job.' The Sarge actually apologised. Carrying the radio was personal.

After a month or two in the bush, men noticed the little things about each other. Like the Aussie bush hats, the giggle hats—or 'Hats Utility', as the Army called them. Utility was right: they were used for lifting a hot mug off a stove, wiping your face, and wiping guk off your rifle. Hats were, like Jacko's radio, personal. Some men would not go into the bush without their hat. Men came close to tears when they were issued a new one after losing the last one in a chopper's downwash, riding on an APC or during contact. Hats were sometimes cut and tailored to be both practical and stylish. Some had the fronts chopped off with a bayonet so the digger could have a full field of vision. Others, in the first years of the war, had a red band threaded through the brim to make sure they weren't mistaken for a Noggie, whose bush hat was similar. Some had messages scrawled on them: the digger's name, their girl's name, *FTA (Fuck The Army)*, *Vietcong Hunting Club* and *I'm A Nasho*. Any writing was done on the back of the hat, of course, to avoid providing a bullseye for Charlie.

Bob Wood noticed Butch pull a shaving brush out of his pack to clean his weapon. Australian soldiers were drilled from day one at recruit training to care for their weapon like it was their mother—'Look after your weapon, son, one day it will look after you'. Very true. So at every opportunity, out came the small oil bottle, the four-by-two cleaning rag, the pull-through cord for the barrel, and the shaving brush. After a month you could recognise another soldier's brush. A great mystery of war: why didn't the Army issue a dedicated rifle brush?

Men's backpacks, strapped to fiberglass frames, also took on a personality—maybe held together with hootchie cord and black tape. A new pack made you look like a new guy; and nobody ever wanted that. Likewise with boots: a digger's boots should be well-seasoned, a bit ripped and always covered in mud.

The Goons laid an ambush later that night. Spirits were low; the war was wearing men down. The answer was a Yippee Shoot. The Goons had perfected the Yippee Shoot, an occasion to open up with every weapon in the dark and blast … no-one. Yippee Shoots were dangerous, strictly illegal, and a great laugh. Bob Wood, Dixie, Boodgie and Butch held their own Orders Group and carefully planned it. Every Goon was in on it—except the Sarge and the commander. Sarge suspected that the last three or four 'firefights' were Yippees, and had made growling noises about charging 'the next bastard I catch having an accidental discharge in the bush. You can blow the eardrums out of your mates and let Charlie know exactly where you are. The war's winding down, but the Nogs aren't!'

At a track junction the Goons hunkered down and formulated the plan. 'Go!' hissed Dixie, and Wood was up and running parallel to the track for 50 metres in the dark. He waited until Dixie had disarmed the trip wire flare in front of the ambush before struggling to get his boots off. The plan involved Wood running back along the track barefoot—like the enemy. Even Einstein wouldn't guess the footprints were Wood's size-nine feet. The commander would check the track in the morning light after the ambush had been strung and look for footprints. A Yippee Shoot had to look and sound real, or there'd be a full investigation back at the Dat.

One boot off and bending to unlace the other, Wood heard Dixie's low whistle. *Fuck, Sarge must doing the rounds. Checking the ambush.* Wood opted for Plan B and sprinted back, barefoot on the sandy track and booted foot in the bush. *I hope the boys know I'm on my way back or I'll get zapped. Hope like hell Charlie doesn't come round the bend and see a one-booted Aussie hopping like a kangaroo ...* Wood reached Dixie's position and dived into the bush so as not to leave footprints right into the ambush position.

'Okay, let her go!' Dixie nudged Butch on the M60, and there was a deafening roar as a hail of fire tore down the track, tracers flicked through the air. Fifty metres of jungle was trashed. Each man expended a full magazine into the blackness, grinning and cackling at the fabulous din.

Fire Base Ziggie was up and running. The 105 howitzers were bedded in and had pounded the surrounding area with H and I fire. The rifle companies were out searching for enemy and Doggy Dwyer was out on ambush—his fourth in as many days. His humour had deserted him. He had three days left in-country, and should have been worried about getting zapped so close to RTA—every short-timer's nightmare—but he wasn't. He was seriously pissed off instead.

Each day as he walked out through the wire with the platoon, a chopper flew in with hot box meals. On fire bases the hot box was delivered from the Dat to provide a hot meal—chicken, steak, mashed potato, peas, carrots, even custard and fruit. Sometimes a fresh-baked roll. Doggy and his section had missed the hot meal for the past three days. Instead, he'd been chewing on dry biscuits and tasteless US ham slices out of a can. Dwyer thought conspiracies. *There they sit in their sandbagged bunkers surrounded by walls of wire, eating hot food, crapping on long-drop toilets, wiping their arses with toilet paper, reading books, listening to AFVN Radio and showering under the canvas buckets we strung up yesterday. And we lay here on our guts waiting for Charlie.*

The next day, after an all-night ambush, Dwyer led the platoon back in through the wire—just as the hot box special touched down. The food was doled out by servers into the soldier's aluminum Dixie dish under the supervision of officers and senior NCOs. Dwyer and the others from Anti-Tank platoon, filthy, red-eyed and dead-tired, grabbed their Dixies and bounded up to the queue, where men were salivating. *I'd kill for a hot meal—a piece of roast chicken, though, not that boiled, grey steak.*

Dwyer reached the server. 'Chicken, thanks mate,' he said. 'I could eat the arse out of an Afghan's underpants.'

A lieutenant suddenly stepped forward and covered the hot container with chicken in it. 'No chicken left, have the steak.'

Dwyer looked at the hot box and then up at the officer. 'Chicken, thanks.'

'No chicken left, soldier, move on.'

Dwyer folded his Dixie and took one last look at the officer before walking back to his weapon pit, where he tore open a ration pack and munched a biscuit. *I've never felt hatred like this before. That bastard broke the Soldier's Code—the diggers eat first. That fucker has taken food orders from his brother officers, and I wanted their piece of chicken. That fucker is going to die—now!*

Dwyer carefully and quietly removed the magazine from his Armalite and slipped out a bullet. He held the 5.56mm round in his hand. He breathed on it, rubbed it on his cruddy shirt, and slid it back into the magazine.

One sip of coffee, up and walk over to him. About 10 feet should do it. He must see me and I must tell him, he's broken the Soldier's Code. Dwyer cocked the rifle and began to stand. *Bullet straight to the head or chest. He must see it coming …*

A hand pushed firmly down on his shoulder.

'Doggy, mate, you look crook.' He turned to see his section commander standing over him. The man bent and spoke quietly.

'Been watching ya, Doggy. You're out the day after tomorrow and I reckon you deserve a rest. Take a break off gun sentry tonight and I'll do it for you, mate.'

The two men looked at each other, the section commander spoke again. 'Well, you lucky short-timer bastard, you gonna make me a bloody brew or not? And no salt, thanks mate.'

BLOOD AND THUNDER

Wilf Matusch watched while each man reached the edge of the swamp, then stepped out with that curious gawky, balancing step when you can't see what's under your feet. It was like the newsreels he'd seen as a youngster, black-and-white clips of World War II diggers in New Guinea holding their weapons above the water and gingerly trying to walk in the footsteps of the man in front. Matusch stepped into the green and black water and looked ahead towards the forward scouts, Hobbo and Shorty Mawer, who almost disappeared beneath the scum before reaching the bank and scrambling out to do a check of the thick bush. Mawer returned to the edge of the swamp and gave the thumbs-up—all clear.

All 28 men made the high ground and melted into the jungle in single file. A short while later, after skirting a track junction and now on firm ground, Platoon Commander Alcock called an extended lunch break. A quick clearing patrol checked the surrounding jungle, sentries were posted, and men brewed up and heated cans of American rations. Matusch looked around—he felt comfortable with the unit. *We're seasoned warriors now. Months in Vietnam and we know what we are doing. Each man knows what's required of him.* He sipped his brew and re-read a letter from Lyn, the girl he was going to marry when he got home. *Got home?* The thought came and went in a flash.

Alcock and Shorty Mawer had been listening to the races on Australian Armed Forces Radio and were discussing their win/loss status. The atmosphere was quiet and peaceful, broken only by a *clink* and *clunk* as each man finished his coffee and snapped shut the steel handle on his mug. Minutes later, Alcock called the section commanders in and gave them another brief. 'The mission is to recce an enemy camp about here,' he stabbed a finger at the map spread on the ground. 'We'll scout, and if it looks good we'll put an assault in tomorrow.'

The soldiers hauled on their packs. *We can handle a fight, no worries,* thought Matusch, studying the M79 grenade launchers, M72 rocket launchers and extra belts of ammunition each man was swinging across his backpack. Then there were the Assault Pioneers to check for mines and booby-traps, and the Forward Air Controller to call in air strikes. *We're ready as we're ever going to be to kick Charlie's arse.*

Alex, the radio operator, finished sending crypto-encoded messages to company headquarters, including the platoon's locstat and latest sitrep. The national serviceman carried his codes in a plastic-covered 'vui tui'—a small photo album with plastic inserts sold by traders in the Vung Tau. The 'vui tui' also held the standard procedures for requesting maintenance and operational demands, artillery or mortar support, dustoff and the numerous other reports that were required on a daily basis. Alex was given instructions and messages by his platoon commander, which he would scribble on plastic with a chinograph pencil before encoding them and passing them on over the radio. The radio, a 25 set, was strapped on his back with his pack. The signaller was one of the most loaded-down men in the war: in addition to his normal Infantry equipment and kit, he also carried the radio, spare batteries and a complete set of antennae.

Alcock stood, swung his pack onto his back and nodded to his men to do the same. Shorty Mawer, the scout, pushed his way into the bush and was soon swallowed by bamboo and a cargo net of vines. The platoon began to bunch up as they do when getting ready to move. Alcock put five fingers up, closed his fist, then flashed five fingers again—ten paces between each man. The signal went back down the line. The men began to bunch again. Matusch waited for his turn to move out, standing an arm's length from Alcock. *We're bunching, shouldn't do that, too close to each—*

There was a sudden red flash surrounded by a black halo behind Alcock. Mawer—as switched on as any scout—swung his rifle through his arc of responsibility. He searched the low ground, the middle ground … *crack-whoomp!* He was blown off his feet. He rolled and jumped up again before spinning around. 'What the hell was that?' He pushed his way back into the platoon position and gaped at the carnage. Matusch was kneeling on the ground, head in the leaves, hands over his face like a man praying to Mecca.

Alex was slumped on the ground, holding the radio handset in his right hand. His left hand was hanging limp below what looked like a sandwich-sized bite that had taken away nearly all of his wrist. He was rapidly turning white. His training kicked in as he spoke urgently but calmly into the handset. Above the ringing in his ears, Matusch heard Alex send the message: '6:1, we have mines, we have casualties, we need dustoff. More to follow. Wait out.' The transmission was top priority—all others should cease unless equally urgent.

Alcock was trying to reach up behind his back, which had been buckshot with shrapnel. Bushman Scout Tihn was staring in disbelief at his own hand: two fingers were missing. Mawer heard the screams from Assault Pioneer and long-time mate, Toby, writhing among leaf litter. 'Argh, help me. Help me!' Men twisted on the ground, knelt, covered their ears, stood and swayed with mouths gaping, dumbfounded with shock.

Matusch leaned back on his calves and pulled off his pack. *What's that? Sounds like someone's emptying a water bottle on the ground. Wait—it's not water, it's blood.* For a second he watched, fascinated by the blood gushing from his face like ink squirting from a fountain pen. The booby-trap was only metres from where the men had eaten their lunch. An Assault Pioneer called Greg had trodden on the torch battery-powered bamboo trigger, which caused the two wires to complete a circuit, detonating the device. The blast didn't go up, it went sideways—just as it was designed to do. Greg's foot was vaporised in the blast. Red-hot metal fragments—nails and pieces of shrapnel scrap from allied bombs and artillery rounds—shot up and out in a deadly scything arc. A chunk of APC steel track chopped straight through Alex's wrist. Other fragments hit Tihn and Alcock. The shockwave shattered Toby's legs in five places, breaking both femurs and tibias. The digger panted for oxygen between screams of agony.

Matusch held his hands to his face in an attempt to stem the blood now streaming down. He could see only red. He grabbed at his mate, John Bolste. 'John, I've lost my eye!'

'No, no—you're right, you've just got a bloody big hole in your face, that's all.'

Matusch suddenly remembered he was the medic. He jammed his filthy sweat rag into his eye socket.

'Don't be a dickhead Wilf, put a shell dressing over it.' Bolste pulled Matusch's blood-covered hands clear and, with a bayonet, sliced through the shell dressing taped to the rifle butt. He yanked away the protective coating and unravelled a yard of gauze and an 8 x 4-inch padded dressing, then helped wrap it around his mate's face.

Alcock, still shaking with shock, tried to take control of the situation. 'Mines! Freeze! We're in a minefield. Don't anyone move. Use your bayonets, probe, *probe!* Casualties, how many casualties?'

Alex was back on the radio as the section commanders called their casualty stats. Eleven men down, most serious. 'This is 6:1, over. We have 11 Whiskey India Alpha. Over. We have two lying wounded, nine sitting wounded. Request urgent dustoff. Urgent. Over.'

At BHQ the message was relayed to Task Force and on to Vung Tau, where Vampire Hospital had dustoff Hueys on standby. Casualty evacuation procedure was listed alphabetically, each letter giving vital information. Alex checked his 'vui tui' and spoke into the handset:

'Alpha [map reference]: Grid 476098.

Bravo [status]: Urgent.

Charlie [condition of wounded]: Two lying, nine sitting.

Delta [number of wounded]: 11 WIA.

Echo [type of wounds]: Leg, arm, hand, chest, head.

Foxtrot [radio frequency]: No change.

Golf [equipment needed to get wounded out]: Winch, litter, penetrator.

Hotel [likelihood of enemy attack]: Secure.

India [other special requirements]: Nil.'

BHQ requested more information. The signaller, one hand almost detached from his arm and fighting back the nausea, spoke again, 'We require litters, we are in a minefield, we have lost our mine-clearing equipment ... we can't clear an LZ. Sunray suggests winching the wounded out. Over.' His duty done, the radioman fell back and stared at his mangled hand.

Matusch was rummaging through his medical kit and throwing shell dressings and bandages to the other men, who were frantically using their bayonets to probe the ground for mines, and clearing safe paths to the wounded. He answered the urgent queries.

'Wilf, where do I tie off ...?'

'Wilf, what the fuck do I do with this thing?'

His head was spinning as he called back. 'Push it up. *Right into the groin* ... Splint ... use a bloody splint on the ankle, wrap your shirt around it, I'll get to you soon as I can ...'

Alex tied a tourniquet around his upper arm and then began to check his 'vui tui' for in-bound dustoff protocol. Men shouted out the nature and seriousness of their wounds while Alex scribbled notes with his good hand. Johnny Bolste suddenly erupted with fury, lifting his rifle and advancing on Tihn. '*Fuck you*, your bloody mates did this. I'm going to shoot you, you fucking turncoat.' As Bolste lifted the rifle to his shoulder, Matusch grabbed him around the waist and pushed the rifle down and away before it discharged.

'S'okay, s'okay, he's hit too, the poor bastard.'

Matusch wrapped Tihn's hand, then shoved Bolste, who was still glaring at the Bushman Scout. 'Check Alex's hand.'

Bolste looked up, then away. 'Can't, mate, your face is bad enough …'

The thought of terrible disfigurement went through Matusch's mind. *I'm gonna be like the Phantom of the Opera, wearing a bloody mask for the rest of my days. But still no pain. Maybe I'm going to die suddenly. Everything is still red …*

Matusch knelt next to Alex. 'Let me see your arm. I want to dress it.'

'Piss off, Wilf, don't waste your time. It's fucked.'

'How can you be sure? Let the doctors decide …'

'Take another good look, Wilf.'

Alex smiled weakly. Matusch looked like a Sikh with a blood-soaked turban around his head and over his right eye. 'You're the medic. Tell me, honestly, it won't have to come off.'

Three dustoff helicopters were speeding to the blast site. The pilots were picking up the transmissions from Call Sign 6:1. While the door gunners and flight medics prepared for the casualty evacuation, the pilots confirmed the situation with the platoon radio operator.

'6:1, this is dustoff. Over.'

Alex flicked his radio to 'Squelch' so he could answer. There was no need for coding: '6:1 Roger. Send.'

'Inbound your location. Over.' The pilot scanned the notes on his kneepad to confirm he had all the information for what lay ahead. Alex dropped his head, exhausted and relieved: the dustoffs were close. He had passed on all the details needed to get his mates out. He pulled the handset back to his ear and pressed the 'Pressle' switch. 'Roger. Out.'

The situation came under control again as training procedures clicked in. Security was the main priority. Alcock had rallied his men and positioned those uninjured by the blast in the other two section areas. He'd secured the casualty zone by establishing a defensive perimeter. *We're soldiers, we know what to do. Keep the men active, break the shock cycle.* With M60s covering likely enemy approaches, Alcock was reasonably confident he could hold off a ground assault. He selected a winch area for the wounded beneath an opening in the canopy.

The thud of the dustoffs came in across the trees and the familiar red cross was soon visible overhead. Matusch helped place Toby in the canvas litter with splints down both sides. He winced when he checked the Pioneer's ankle—the foot was dangling by a thin strand of skin. He grabbed a toggle rope and tied the foot to the lower leg to stop it falling off. The crewman above hit the winch button and Toby was gently lifted up through the trees. Suddenly the downwash shook the toggle rope loose and it dangled, twisting in the wind.

'Oh shit.' Matusch prayed it wouldn't snag a tree. He recalled the lecture during medic training: if the litter gets caught and the aircraft is in danger, explosive bolts are triggered and the half-inch cable severed. In his mind's eye Matusch saw the litter stall, heard the bang as the crewman fired the charge, and ... He could see the pilot peering out the window, nudging his aircraft forwards and backwards, the landing skids almost touching the trees. *Are these blokes any good, or what?*

Greg, with his missing foot, went next, and the first chopper backed away. Like a taxi rank, the next dustoff moved into position to take its load and the jungle penetrators came down.

Alex was still at his radio post. There was a crackle and hiss as BHQ requested an update. APCs were coming to take the rest of the men out. The mission was over.

The second Huey was loaded with wounded, including Alex, and the third lined up for the final lift. It was Matusch's turn to get on the penetrator seat. Bolste pushed the exhausted medic towards the lift-off spot. Matusch was concerned about his pack and his leather-bound compendium with Lyn's letters.

'Get the hell out, Wilf, I'll take care of this shit for you.'

Matusch clung to the cable and looked down. The last he saw of his platoon were the faces of Bolste and Shorty Mawer looking up at him.

Fire Support Base Ziggie, mid-afternoon, and the Iroquois came clattering in with the daily resup and hot box run. Soon men were unloading cartons of rations, jerry cans, boxes of ammunition and spare equipment ordered by the tankies and APC crews, who were always breaking something important.

The aircraft unloaded, the door gunner gave the thumbs-up and Doggy Dwyer trotted forward, head down and climbed into the seat with his back to the pilot. *Out. Out of the war and soon out of Vietnam. And in one piece.* He watched the door gunner tilt the M60 upwards and go on alert as the Huey banked and turned over the firebase. *Vietnam—Alert—Alive. Don't ever switch off.* The dirty brown of the base faded to jungle green. There was cool, clean air. Dwyer looked up at the blue sky and down at the narrow, brown watercourses. The jungle looked so … natural. Natural, yes … neutral, never. He felt a soothing wave of relief, then a pang of guilt about leaving his mates. He was going; they were staying.

THE NIGHT SURFER

The third Huey headed south to Vung Tau some minutes behind the other two. Wilf Matusch sat next to another of the platoon's wounded, 'Bird' Cleary. There was blood on the man's uniform but Matusch was incapable of focusing on any of Cleary's actual wounds.

'You okay, Wilf?' Cleary was leaning over and looking at the medic's head dress. Matusch was feeling his face, pushing into the eye socket to check if he still had an eyeball. *It feels like an eye but it's hard to tell because most of my face is numb ...*

The dustoffs landed and transferred their wounded to the medical teams crouching beneath the rotors' downwash. The waiting wheelchairs and litters on castor wheels were quickly filled. Concerned orderlies moved among the wounded, checking dogtags, taking names, ranks and serial numbers, and confirming blood groups. Matusch felt someone cutting away his boots, trousers and shirt. He was aware of the stinking muck, blood and sweat that covered his filthy body. *Hell, a while ago we were up to our armpits in swamp water. I must smell like a shot fox.*

An orderly bent over him. 'What have we here ... cuts, nicks. We'll have you out in the bush with your mates again in a couple of weeks, no worries.'

Hell, no! It's the second time I've been bloody blown up in ten days. Surely I'm cut up enough to get a homer?

Soon a doctor was leaning over him, poking into the hole just below his eye. 'If it had been a little higher, it would have been both eyes, son.'

Flashback: Wilf Matusch—A Canungra lesson: if you stop, go down. When you're on patrol and you stop, go down, even it it's only on one knee. Don't bunch—one burst of enfillade fire will hit everyone; one mine or booby-trap'll get you all. Always spread out, avoid the instinct to bunch up. Never mind what they do in the movies. No John Wayne shit. When you stop, go down. When you move, spread, don't bunch …

'You've got bone fragments in there,' the doctor continued. 'We're busy, but we'll get a head X-ray done.' He moved quietly away.

After the X-ray, Matusch was back in the hall and starting to doze off when suddenly the ward doors burst open with an attendant pointing at a startled Matusch. 'Get this man cleaned up. We've got a chopper coming in fifteen minutes to take him up to Long Binh. He needs a neurosurgeon, quickly.'

Matusch shot up. *They talking about me?* Two orderlies leaned over him—'Wriggle your toes, squeeze my fist. What's your mother's maiden name? What date did you enlist? How are you feeling, soldier?'

A padre approached and Matusch heard the doctor speaking to him. 'This man has shrapnel in the base of his skull, lodged up against his pituitary gland.' The padre bent, looked into the wounded man's face and smiled.

The place was Reservoir Street, Port Kembla on an August day. A telegram was delivered by two Army officers to the home of Matusch's mother, Cornelia.

```
IT IS LEARNED WITH REGRET THAT YOUR SON 217789
PRIVATE WILFRED LEOPOLD MATUSCH WAS PLACED ON
THE SERIOUSLY ILL LIST ON 8TH AUGUST 1970 AT 24
UNITED STATES EVACUATION HOSPITAL LONG BINH VIET-
NAM AS A RESULT OF WOUNDS SUSTAINED IN ACTION IN
PHUOC TUY PROVINCE VIETNAM STOP A PROGRESS REPORT
WILL BE FORWARDED TO YOU AT REGULAR INTERVALS BUT
IF A CHANGE IN CONDITION OCCURS YOU WILL BE NOTI-
FIED IMMEDIATELY … ARMY HEADQUARTERS
```

It took twelve months for Sergeant Jimmy Griffiths to recuperate sufficiently to call himself a soldier ready for service again. His right shoulder had been broken twice during treatment after his plaster and patch-up job at Long Binh. But the veteran figured he should be thankful things weren't a lot worse than an arm bent a bit out of shape. *That was no-one's fault—the Yanks saved my life.* And there was a funny side to his injuries: telling the story.

'Hey Jimmy, you got cut up in Vietnam. Where was that?'

'Operation Overlord. A rifle company hit a bunker full of Nogs.'

'What happened to you?'

'I was in an ammo resup when the chopper got blasted at 120 feet—crashed and burned.'

'So what happened to you?'

'Broke a shitload of bones.'

'Yeah? Lucky you survived the crash.'

'I didn't ... I fell out before it crashed.'

Griffiths had survived the plunge, but not military protocol. He'd lost his pistol—a 9mm Browning—in the tumble and fall. The interrogation about where the Browning went had haunted him ever since.

'Did you conceal the weapon on yourself after the fall?'

'No.'

'Did you arrange to have it smuggled out of the country on the medivac flight?'

'No.'

'Perhaps you secretly slipped the pistol to another man on the ground during your treatment at the contact site to hide and pick up later?'

'Not that I can remember, sir. Almost every bone in my body was smashed up at the time ...'

The Goon Platoon was still settling and checking their wire-laying work when the sergeant passed the word down—ambush tonight. He heard the collective whinge, but had something else on his mind that day: his platoon commander, Dennis Tyson, had picked up a bad stomach bug. He doubled over with pain whenever he stopped for a break on patrol, and he groaned at night. He didn't complain, and no-one knew that at times he felt like he was dying.

The sergeant watched as Tyson took out a recce party to check the ambush site. On his return, they studied the map together and ran a final check on gun and mortar support DFs in case they snagged a sizeable enemy force. The track they selected mean-dered through thick jungle and crossed a creek. It was a sitter for the VC to use: Tyson had noticed the track led to high ground from where FSB Ziggie could be observed. 'If we move in early enough, we might catch them moving along the track back to their bunker system or base camp.' Tyson was barely able to gasp out the words due to the pain.

The soldiers moved out with Butch taking the lead and with Bob Wood carrying the M60 behind Dixie, his section com-mander. Tyson, using a deception plan, took the patrol in an entirely different direction to where the ambush was to be set. Once they entered the jungle, they propped for about 30 minutes and listened to check they weren't being were followed. The patrol then wheeled and, shortly before last light, moved close to the track and creek junction. Tyson took three men with him to do a final recce then sent one back to the sergeant to bring the ambush group forward.

'Dixie, Claymores out—usual bank of four.' The sergeant quietly whispered instructions about the killing ground limits and the problem of flank protection in a linear ambush along a track, particularly with a manpower shortage.

Been here, done it all before, he thought, pulling on a last smoke before settling in. *This mob's like having my own bloody kids, for Chrissake, I've gotta tell 'em everything, down to the last detail. I have to watch them like kids—if there was a railway track around here they'd find it and play on it. What the hell am I going on about—they are kids. Nineteen-, 20-year-olds, surfies, bank clerks, bushies—young men still asking themselves what the bloody hell they're doing over here. What a bunch of whackers—what a bunch of bloody great blokes. Tell 'em to climb the Warbies and take on a bunch of NVA, they'd do it, even though they'd grizzle the whole bloody way. They take the shit and just keep on taking it. We get every crap job in the battalion—walk further, lay more wire, set more bloody ambushes. They just keep on taking it …*

The Goons laid Claymore mines in banks, each mine linked to the next with detonator cord so that they'd all explode together when set off. You relied on surprise, threw a deadly wall of fire at anyone in the killing ground, and made sure your arse was covered. The last thing you want in any ambush, and particularly a linear ambush, is the enemy racing back up the track and counter attacking you from a flank. The Sarge knew things could go awry: during his first tour in '66 he'd been part of an ambush that sprung a group of NVA. On that occasion the enemy reacted aggressively, and in a matter of seconds had turned the ambush around to the point where he and his platoon ended up fighting for their lives. Excellent leadership by his commander and great use of artillery was all that stopped them being overrun.

The sergeant instructed that a minimum of three Claymores be placed on each flank and the rear. *Not much else we can do, but wait and hope a battalion of Nogs heading for Ziggie doesn't come down this road tonight.* Other than being rolled up by Ho Chi Minh's hordes, the greatest danger in an ambush was everyone falling asleep. Protocols called for each man to stay awake, but there was a snowflake's chance in hell of that; everyone was already exhausted. The Goons adopted a 50 percent 'stand to' with men in pairs, where one slept while the other stayed awake, alternating through the night. But there was still the possibility that every soldier might be off with the fairies before midnight.

It was pitch black. The sergeant tossed and turned on a bed of leaves, ignoring the mosquitoes now sucking the blood out of him. *But that leech on my eyelid is dead meat when I get it off. Toss and turn and look into the dark again. If these bastards pull another Yippee Shoot tonight, I'm gonna charge every one of them. Buggers thought I'd fall for the one-legged VC stunt.*

An hour later, out of the darkness came the most blood-curdling scream the sergeant had ever heard—'He's got me! Help me. He's got my leg, stab him, stab the bastard. Quick—heeeelp!'

Every Goon sat bolt upright. The sergeant grabbed his Armalite and spun around in the direction of the sound. *Bloody Nogs are cutting one of my digger's throats!* 'What the fuck's going on over there?'

There were muffled grunts, whispers, the sound of a slap. Then a voice shouted back—'S'all right, Sarge. Butch was having a nightmare. He was surfing and a monkey grabbed his leg …'

The sergeant dropped his head back onto the webbing. *I need another life. What was I thinkin', comin' back here for head-fucks like this? Duty, unfinished business? Prove I was a good leader? Duty-free shopping …?*

'Sarge, Sarge, you there?' A voice in the blackness.

'Course I'm bloody here, where else would I be having all this fun? Who's that?'

It was Tyson, obviously in extreme pain. 'Do you reckon we should get out with all that screaming?' he asked.

'Shit, no. If the Nogs heard that, they'd reckon their bloody ancestors had come back. If we move now, half of Phuoc Tuy will hear us … go to sleep, get some kip.'

Next morning the Goons made their way back to FSB Ziggie. Wood and Boodgie were giving Butch hell.

'You shoulda kept quiet, Butch, you could have had her all to yourself.'

'Hey, Butch, she'd probably have been all right after you gave her a shave.'

'Jeepers, Butch, give the monkey a go, she probably loved your little hairy legs.'

'Mighta been Tarzan, Butch, thought you were Jane.'

By the time the Goons reached the perimeter wire, Butch had got over the sulks and was cuffing and kicking at his mates. Wood and Boodgie just cackled back and dodged Butch's swinging boot like kids in a playground. The sergeant remembered back in '66 when one of the men in his section had to wake him up during a nightmare in the jungle. 'Blood, blood, I'm covered in blood, I'm covered in it!' he'd screamed. That's what this country did to you. It wasn't funny.

He turned as the group filed through the barbed wire. 'Knock it off, fun's over. No more monkeying around.'

That afternoon, Lieutenant Tyson was medivaced to Nui Dat. The sergeant reluctantly became platoon commander.

A SPOT OF BRAIN SURGERY

On his last day in Vietnam, Doggy Dwyer fell out of a Land-Rover.

'You okay, mate? Sorry.' The driver had taken a sharp right instead of left, and with no doors on Land-Rovers in Vietnam, the scout was suddenly airborne. He crash-landed in the dirt, rolled, stood up and put a curse on the driver. After dusting down, he picked up his rifle and made his way to his tent.

He sat on the cot in the platoon lines and felt a blanket of loneliness swamp him. His mates were still out in the field. No-one to talk to, have a laugh with. He avoided the base personnel and busied himself packing and polishing his shoes. *How many months ago did I sit here and get told to carry that useless gun on patrol? Then the radio ... how long ago?* He pulled out the bits and pieces he had stored over the months, the debris of a tour of duty shoved under the cot in a plastic wash basin: a Zippo with the guts removed, a broken watchband, a packet of almost white chocolate, an old thong covered in mud, a box of waterproof matches and a folded card eaten away by mould. He examined the card under the tent's single light bulb.

'Australian Force Vietnam POW Instruction Card
1. As a member of the Australian Army in Vietnam you are required to comply with the Geneva Prisoner of War Convention of 1949 to which your country adheres.'

There were three instructions: disarm the prisoner of war; do not humiliate him; and ensure he is protected against curiosity and reprisals.

Dwyer remembered the Vietnamese banana cutter. He turned the card over and read:

'Key Phrases—

Halt ... *Dung lai*

Lay down your gun ... *Dung sung xuong*

Put up your hands ... *Dua tay len*

Do not talk … *Dung noi chuyen*
Turn right … *Xay ben phai*
Turn left … *Xay ben trai'*

The scout studied the words and remembered the day he'd nearly shot the suspected VC. But there was something about the card that didn't seem right—*Of course: I can't speak bloody Vietnamese.* Also in the washbasin were two War Picture Library Comics—'training manuals', the diggers called them. Dwyer's favourite was 'Sergeant Rock'.

Flashback: Doggy Dwyer—The platoon Looey is looking at the map spread on the ground, plotting grid references, working out the bearings between each, selecting a route over the terrain with my section commander. 'Up here for three clicks, across to this point, I reckon … 'bout two clicks.' I sidle up and peer at the map. 'Do you really think so, sir?' The looey looks up with an indignant expression. 'Why not, Doggy?'

I get down on my haunches and squint then mumble out of the side of my mouth. 'Sergeant Rock, sir, would take the alternative, along the ridgeline.'

I walk away and hear the Looey. 'That bloke's gotta go home, mate. He's been here too long … and who the hell's Sergeant Rock?'

Dwyer put on his polyester uniform and shiny black shoes. He clipped the AUSTRALIA insignia to his epaulettes; and finally, on with the slouch hat, which had been wrapped in plastic. He hitched a ride down to Luscombe Field, and a baby Herc took him to Saigon, where he boarded a Qantas Boeing 707.

Reservoir Street, Port Kembla and the same two uniformed officers who called with the previous telegram were back at the home of Cornelia Wheatley, Wilf Matusch's mother.

STILL SERIOUSLY ILL STOP. IT IS LEARNED THAT THE CONDITION OF YOUR SON 217789 PRIVATE WILFRED LEOPOLD MATUSCH ON 14 AUGUST 1970 IS STILL SERIOUSLY ILL BUT IMPROVING ... ARMY HEAD-QUARTERS.

The Carpenters' song, 'Close to You', drifted through the heavy bandages to the man in the hospital bed. Matusch opened his eyes to see a huge black Staff Sergeant in front of him. 'What time's it?'

There was a wide grin and a row of perfect white teeth. 'Yo' still with us, buddy? Well thank the Lord. Been pretty unsociable, y'know—sleepin', sayin' nuthin for three days.'

A tray appeared—hash browns and apricots. Matusch looked at the food and then around the room. 'Hey mate, where the bloody hell am I and how long have I been here?'

'Yo in Long Binh, 24 Evacuation Hospital, Neurosurgery Ward. Three days now y'all been with us. Don't worry, Ossie, yo goin' be jus' fine.'

What the hell had happened in three days? He tried to backtrack.

The sun was shining directly on him through the window of the Huey during the flight from Vung Tau. It was as hot as hell. Next, a babble of voices, a temperature change and questions—'What's your name, soldier? What's your social security number?'

Matusch managed to whisper what he thought the Americans needed. 'My name is Private Matusch. I don't have a social security number, I have a regimental number.'

'No shit, you an Ossie? Where you from in Oz?'

There were hands on him now. 'Buddy, gotta keep real still for me while I do this X-ray for the doctor … I'm tellin' you, I heard of them big bronzed Anzac Aussies, but you look pretty ridiculous, like yo' been worked over with a goddamn meat axe.'

Then Matusch faded into unconsciousness.

'Hey, man, sit up now—we gonna give you a haircut.' Minutes later: 'Now we gonna put a tube in so you don't wet yourself under anesthetic …'

Sleep again.

'Hey man, you see the bed over there? Tha's right. We gonna put you right there, buddy.' Two men lift and he's back in the ward bed. Sleep, then voices again. 'Hey buddy, we gonna lift you from the bed back onto this here stretcher, ready for another operation …'

Matusch panicked. 'No, no, you got the wrong man—I've had my oper …'

'We know that, man. You gotta have another one while you still so strong. Hold me here …'

Deep sleep. Then pain—needle pain. Each buttock, twice a day. Eventually Matusch begged them to put the needles, which resembled a mini-jackhammer, in his arm. The American nurse smiled. 'Big Anzac you may be, mister. But this in your arm would *really* hurt. Roll over.'

Some time later Matusch felt a scraping. *Shit, some bastard's ripping my face off.* He was being shaved in preparation for the coming operation.

The Carpenters' song came back. Dr Capp, one of the world's top neurosurgeons, was sitting on the edge of Matusch's bed explaining the operations.

'We did several operations on you, beginning with a bone flap to the right side of your head. We drilled four burr holes before we cut your skull to remove the right-hand side of it to get at the shrapnel. We went in and out as quickly as possible, we didn't look around in there on the basis of, if it's working, don't fix it. Then we put your skull back together. There are 27 silver staples in there permanently. We pulled the skin and ear back into place and stitched it so the incision is above your hairline—you won't see the scar when the hair grows back.'

Later, Matusch was told that the piece of shrapnel they removed was only about half the size of a pea, but if left untreated it would certainly have either killed him or turned him into a cabbage. Capp had just a week left of his tour in the war zone—Matusch was lucky.

Letters from home were forwarded to the patient from Nui Dat— all a week old. A distressed Matusch asked to get a message home to his mother and Lyn, and a nurse sent a telegram through Red Cross in Saigon. Shortly after, a one-page reply arrived from Lyn.

'Dear Wilf,

Your mother phoned me this evening saying she had received a telegram from the Army, delivered in person by two men in uniform. I cried when I heard that you were wounded, your mother cried while she told me how serious the injuries were and I should prepare myself for you to take a long time recovering ...'

Eastern Command Personnel Depot, Watsons Bay, New South Wales, and Doggy Dwyer was already having a blue. The Duty Sergeant, with his World War II ribbons, was yelling at the soldiers, doling out daily duties. The yelling was getting to Dwyer, who couldn't break the habit of whispering. The old bastard's arrogant attitude wasn't helping.

'Dwyer—kitchen duties!'

The veteran felt the hate rise, felt himself going cold. *Vietnam, patrols, no hot food, denied my chicken dinner ...*

Above: A soldier and his friends. 3RAR padmaster, Jimmy Griffiths, befriended members of a Vietnamese orphanage in the town of Dat Do. Griffiths badgered fellow soldiers to contribute towards the welfare of the children, until he was critically injured when an ammunition resupply helicopter, in which he was travelling, was shot down by enemy fire. (J. Griffiths)

Above: Corporal 'Bones' Green, section commander with 7 Platoon 3RAR, follows a swollen creek during search and destroy operations in 1971. (Neil Moody)

Left: 'Goon Platoon' member, 'Boodgie' barely visible in thick country during a patrol in Phuoc Tuy Province. (Bob Wood)

Above and left: Edmund 'Ted' Harrison, a member of 5RAR, suffered horrific wounds from a booby trap grenade during operations in Phuoc Tuy Province in 1966. Harrison was evacuated to Australia where he continued to suffer from the aftermath of the wounding. (E. Harrison)

Left and below: Robert 'Woody' Wood of 7 Platoon 'The Goons' C Coy 3RAR volunteered for National Service. Wood was determined to become an infantry soldier and serve with a combat unit in Vietnam. (Lt Col Peter Scott)

Above: Flight for life. A Dustoff helicopter landing at the 1st Australian Field Hospital's chopper pad (Vampire) at Vung Tau. Note the stretcher attached to the inside of the aircraft passenger bay. (1st Australian Field Hospital Association, courtesy Bob and Denise Bell)

Below: A team of Australian surgeons work on a wounded digger at 1st Australian Field Hospital, Vung Tau. Quick evacuation and skilled medical teams saved countless lives during the Vietnam War. (1st Australian Field Hospital Association)

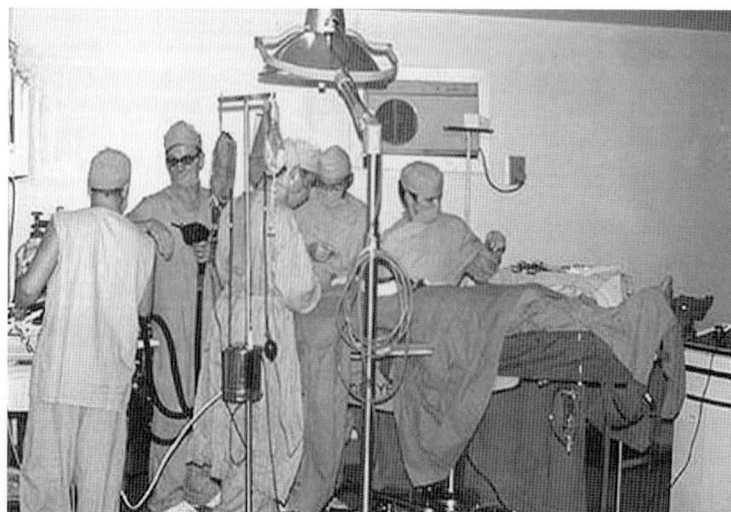

Above: Buggered in the bush...a soldier takes a break during jungle patrol. Fatigue through relentless patrolling was a constant danger during operations in Vietnam. (Garry Davis)

Below: A moment's exchange for a joke and a smoke as C Company's 7 Platoon dismounts and prepares for patrol. Note the 'under and over' M16 rifle with a grenade launcher attached beneath. (Neil Moody)

Above: Lt Col Peter Scott, Commanding Officer, 3 Battalion RAR attempts to drop smoke grenades to his troops who are in heavy enemy contact. Seconds after this photo was taken the helicopter was shot down by enemy fire. (Aub Dwyer)

Below: Sharing a meal and making a brew...soldiers in Vietnam relied on the 'buddy system' with each man helping his mate during day-to-day soldiering. (Garry Davis)

Above: Infantry/armour cooperation up the sharp end. Soldiers and Centurions hunt the Viet Cong in thick vegetation. When soldiers and 'tankies' worked in cooperation a major concern for the infantryman was being run down by the huge battle tank. (W. Matusch)

Right: The back-breaking 'average' load carried by an infantryman. The equipment weighed about 80 pounds and included rations, water, personal equipment and ammunition. The tube-shaped weapon was a light anti-tank device that fired a rocket. The steel helmet was only worn when required, such as during an impending mortar attack, in known minefield areas or on road convoy.
(W. Matusch)

Above: The Aussie digger...Corporal Barry Baker, Section Commander 7 Platoon C Coy 3RAR epitomises the blend of larrikin, rebel, mate and fighter in the ANZAC tradition of his forefathers. (Neil Moody)

Above: The Vietnamese bushman scout assisted the Australian soldier during operations. The scout was often an enemy soldier who defected during the war and joined the Allied Forces. (Garry Davis)

'I'm here for discharge, not bashing Dixies in the bloody mess … I've got procedural responsibilities.'

The older man advanced on the 20-year-old. 'Look here, son, I don't care where you've been or how long you've got left in the Army, it's the OR's Mess and kitchen duties.'

Maybe it was the 'son' that hit the button. Dwyer readied himself for the kill—then realised he had no rifle. He went to the Adjutant's office. There was a discussion, and it was agreed Dwyer would take accrued leave and report in at the Depot on the day of discharge.

It was 0800 hours when the Vietnam veteran arrived for his discharge. By noon his papers were signed and he eyeballed the old sergeant, who sneered, 'You're not officially out of the Army until midnight, soldier.'

They eyed each other off like dogs about to fight. Then the Duty Sergeant jerked his thumb towards the gate. The last words Doggy Dwyer head in the Army were, 'Okay, fuck off.'

Time to get another life, thought Dwyer, scanning the morning papers. Aha! The advertisement said a security company was interested in hiring ex-Army personnel. Of more interest, it stated 'particularly Vietnam veterans'. A day later, Dwyer walked out of the firm's offices not sure whether to laugh or cry. The words of the smartly dressed security consultant still rang in his ears: 'All looks pretty good, Mr Dwyer, but you're too young to carry a gun …'

How about the NSW police force? 'Sorry, you don't meet the height requirement.'

Then a friend said, 'Try the NSW Fire Brigade, it's a good life with the smokies.' In late 1971, ex-chicken de-beaker and forward scout Allan Dwyer became a firefighter.

NIGHT DUSTOFF

Reservoir Street, Port Kembla. An envelope is personally delivered.

Signal to Mrs. C. Wheatley re: Your son, Pte W.L. Matusch, 217789, Vietnam

Through our National Headquarters in Melbourne, we have just received a signal from our Red Cross Unit in Vietnam with a message to you from your son, Pte Matusch. His message reads as follows:

'Unit Vietnam Signals Ref 217789 Pte W.L. Matusch message for mother Mrs. C Wheatley Reservoir Street, Port Kembla. Quote *Dear Mother got a little bit hurt. Am okay. Please tell Lyn Love Wilf* unquote.'

Carmel O'Shea, our Red Cross member there, visited your son at the 24 U.S. Evac Hospital, and she has written to you and to Pte Matusch's girlfriend on his behalf. So you will be reassured to know that mail is definitely on its way … Miss P. Neasbey, Director, National Tracing Bureau.

There were 30 men in the C–130 Hercules medivac; both sides of the plane were lined with stretchers three tiers high. Two doctors and a number of nurses moved among the men. 'How you feeling, okay? Can we adjust that just a bit for you?'

Matusch was classified as 'walking wounded'. Alex, the radio operator, was prostrate and very quiet. So were others, silent for good reason—deep head wounds, chests blown apart and stitched back up. One man had lost his sight.

Matusch's gaze drifted to a digger who looked extremely ill. He had lain on the stretcher without moving all the way from Vung Tau to 4RAAF Camp Hospital in Butterworth, Malaysia. And now, en route to Richmond, near Sydney, he remained perfectly still. He had been fitted up with a tracheotomy; tubes seemed to actually grow from his body and feed into a bundle of oxygen bottles strapped to the fuselage.

Matusch had time to think—to think about that small patch of ground he had walked around, talking with the men on patrol. Alcock and Shorty listening to the races. *We were all so ready to kick arse. And then they booted our arse, right off the top of Mt Everest. That small patch of ground with that fucking obscenity buried in it, they knew we were coming. The cunning bastards knew! One patch of ground above a swamp—where else would you place a booby-trap? God, they wiped out eleven soldiers in one hit, nearly the whole patrol. We were just too arrogant. We thought we knew what we were doing; got careless. One slip, like bunching up, and all the bloody lights go out.*

Alex was moaning softly on his stretcher: pain from the phantom limb. The radioman's hand had to be amputated. He'd been a promising draftsman back in civilian life, back before the government said, 'We need you for this little war we've got going on.' Alex: a dedicated soldier, a Nasho who had hung onto a handset covered in blood to make sure the casevac would come and take his mates out.

Matusch thought about the 'what if's? *What if we had done the right thing and not bunched up? What if Alcock hadn't been standing almost in front of me? I would have taken a lot more shrap in the head. If he had moved a few more inches to the right I wouldn't have been hit at all, maybe* ... Closing his eyes, he saw again the orange flash with the black halo. That second changed his life forever.

The doctors and nurses on the Herc were back near the guy with the tube down his throat, adjusting the oxygen cylinders. A doctor quietly and quickly worked his way to the cockpit. He returned, his face drawn. 'We've got to go to Brisbane ... got a problem.' There was more muttering near the patient, more fiddling with the oxygen. Matusch leaned forward and heard '... it's been leaking all the way. It's nearly run out.'

The Herc dropped, shuddered, then dropped again, descending as quickly as it could without causing more problems for the wounded. The big plane lined up the runway at Brisbane Airport; the men felt the thud as it touched down and rumbled along the strip with a massive engine reverse, jerking and shaking. Emergency vehicles raced alongside. With a series of loud coughs, the engines shut down and an oxygen pipe was passed in. The medical crew bunched around the man with the tube in his throat. Men stared at the drama unfolding; some put their heads in their hands. Save him, save him. *All this bloody way from Vietnam and the oxygen leaks. Got him this far—you've got to save him ...*

The fact that most of his family thought he couldn't walk was a source of some amusement to Wilf Matusch when the bus pulled up outside 2 Camp Military Hospital at Ingleburn. 'We thought you'd be on a stretcher,' were Cornelia's first words. Her son was groggy and most of his head was shaved. His girlfriend, Lyn, had been granted compassionate leave from Teachers College in Armidale and had caught the overnight train to Sydney.

Matusch spent the night in hospital and was allowed to walk in the gardens around the base next morning. He pulled on his uniform and gingerly touched his head. He was getting headaches. There was still fresh scarring on the side of his scalp where the bone had been cut away to get at his brain. He walked outside. *Safe back in Australia. A bit knocked around, but home safe.* A Duty Sergeant emerged from the building opposite. 'Soldier! I'm talking to you, soldier! Get your bloody hat on!'

The Goons were back on night ambush. It was black as a dog's guts and so quiet you could hear the chomper ants having sex. Platoon medic Peter 'Doc' Forbes was certain he had a medical emergency on his hands. He was crawling back in towards

Platoon Headquarters where he thought he could hear the sarge snoring.

'Sarge, Sarge, you there?' Forbes tried to keep his voice down.

The sergeant rolled over. 'No. No, I'm not here, Forbesy, I've pissed off and gone into Hoa Long for a dance. Of course I'm here, you idiot. Wassup?'

Forbes crawled in closer until he bumped into the other's man face. 'Sorry, sorry … it's Davo. I think he's got to go out.'

The sergeant sat bolt upright. *Just getting nicely settled and a digger's gotta go out?* 'Go out bloody where—the Dat Do dogs?'

'Davo's really crook, his temperature's gone off the thermometer. He's beginning to cook.'

There was a moment's silence.

'Forbesy, are you all right? We can't get a dustoff in tonight. Jeez, man, it's pitch black and there just might—just might—be a few Nogs around here. Why the hell didn't you piss 'im off earlier?'

The medic sat back on his heels, and put on his best offended act. 'Well, well … I thought he was getting better.'

The sergeant cursed for another solid minute then kicked out at the radio operator. 'Jacko, Jacko, don't lie there bloody foxing, get Major Tilly on the blower and tell him to stand by. We'll need a jungle penetrator.'

This is a friggin' nightmare. And it's my decision—I'm the platoon commander.

Private Garry Davis had indeed been ill, with almost identical symptoms to Dennis Tyson, including chronic constipation. Doc Forbes had pumped enough laxative into the digger to empty a bull elephant, but Davo had moved nothing more than a string of the loudest farts in Vietnam. *Have we eaten something bad? Been drinking something poisoned? The water from the Song Rai near the Gobi Desert, maybe? Enough chemicals in that to poison a bloody battalion.*

The sergeant pulled the medic close up to his face, whispering, 'Doc, listen. Think carefully about this. It can't wait 'till light, right?'

Forbes shook his head.

The sergeant went on. 'We've got to get a chopper in and get him up through the trees, possibly with VC out there, you know that, right?'

Forbes sat for a moment on his heels, then shook his head. 'Nope, the man's too sick. He's gotta go out.'

This is shaping up to a huge clusterfuck. 'You'd better be right on this one, Doc.'

Jacko was up next to his commander. 'OC's on the blower, Tilly's goin' apeshit. Says we're too far away from each other if the shit hits the fan …'

The sergeant grabbed the handset. 'Shit hits the fan. That's the problem—shit.'

There was more mumbling. By now all the Goons were awake and listening to the drama unfold.

Wood and Boodgie sat up like to two ferrets sniffing the air. 'What's the matter, Sarge? Who's in the shit?'

The sergeant dropped the handset with a grunt. Major Tilly had begrudgingly agreed to the dustoff, but the Sarge had certainly picked up the disapproval in his voice.

'*You're* in the shit, Woody, get your bloody eyes to the front and watch out for Nogs. There'll be a battalion of 'em here in the next half-hour.'

Night dustoff was dangerous in every way: a chopper hammering through the darkness was going somewhere important. The VC would hear it and assess in a heartbeat that it was coming in for a night extraction. The chopper had to locate, almost to the metre, where to hover, then clatter about in the dark for 10 or 15 minutes while the sick man was slowly and carefully winched up. The sergeant had to light the medivac point from the ground. In his mind's eye he saw the green tracer fly upwards, and the chopper shudder as it was hit. Things could be worse, but as he pulled out his pencil flares and designated a couple of Goons to pick a winch site, the platoon sergeant couldn't imagine *much* worse.

Jacko flicked the radio to 'Squelch' and waited for the transmission from the pilot. *Hell, they'll be nice and happy.*

'Three-one, this is inbound dustoff. Sitrep. Over.'

The crackle over the radio sounded like a gunshot in the heat of the Vietnam night. Jacko pulled the handset as close as possible to his mouth to muffle his voice. 'Dustoff, this is 3:1. One man seriously ill. Jungle penetrator. We'll mark. Over.'

The sergeant popped two pencil flares and fired them up through the canopy. There was a *phutt phutt,* then two bright red lights as the flares burst. The noise was deafening as the Huey slowly came to a hover above the trees. Next moment, the pilot flicked on his spotlight and every man on the ground froze with fear.

'Move. Move, bloody *move.'* The sergeant watched as Doc Forbes pulled Davis towards the lift spot and looked up as the chopper crewman lowered the jungle penetrator. The sergeant marvelled for a moment at the skill of the crewman who swung the awkward device left, right, left again through a hole in the canopy that a man could barely squeeze through. The men waited until the penetrator had touched down to allow for the dissipation of its static electricity. Davis was hurriedly placed onto the fold-down prong seat and strapped on.

The sergeant slung the rifle over the sick man's shoulder. 'Hope you won't need this in the next few minutes, Davo!'

Davis kicked branches out of the way as the agonisingly slow upward winch began.

Don't tangle, please don't tangle. If there were shots now they'd fire the bolts and Davo would fall. That'd fix up his no-shit problem once and for all.

The Goon was pulled inboard, and with a crackle—'Roger. Patient on board. Well done, gentlemen. Over'—the dustoff banked and pulled up and away at full throttle.

The sergeant told the Goons to pack. 'We've gotta move now, Nogs'll know we're here. I'm tellin' you blokes, every man in this platoon will, from this day on, shit every day. I kid you not ... and I will be checking ...'

AFTERBURN

He'd left for Vietnam on Mother's Day, May 8, 1966, only 19 years and 28 days old. He'd travelled by Qantas 707, and was in the toilet, sick, most of the way. When he flew back seven months later, he was again sick—very sick, bandaged up like a mummy.

Ted Harrison will always remember October 17, 1966 with absolute clarity, when, on the slopes of the Nui Thi Vai he nearly drowned in his own blood. He drifted beyond the pain into another dimension, where he knew his life was slipping away. *Slap, slap!* More pain, this time across his face. 'Doc' Tony White, the RMO of 5th Battalion, was slapping him about the face to bring him back. Then morphine and a beautiful sleep.

Harrison thought things couldn't get any worse than being blown up. But they could and, for the young soldier, they did. He had not written to his mates in 5RAR. There were reasons: he had been very sick, and then went into post-traumatic shock. He was also racked by guilt at leaving them. He studied the newspapers: it was the usual hyperbole, telling people in Australia nothing about what was really happening over there.

Australian Troops in Heavy Action against Cong—AAP Two Australians were killed and six wounded in Vietnam at the weekend.

Stiff Fighting for Diggers in Vietnam—AAP-Special: Australian troops have run into stiff Vietcong resistance in a sweep through thick jungle country honeycombed with bunkers about 20 miles north of Nui Dat …

Diggers Kill 59 Enemy Troops—Saigon, Wed, AAP— Australian Task Force troops killed 59 Vietcong in an Allied offensive …

What jabbed him like a knife were the reports of the WIA. Correspondents sitting in an air-conditioned bureau office in

Saigon wrote home, 'Allied casualties were light, with three Australians WIA ... 'There were no faces to the story: a man lying bleeding, believing this was the place he'd die—in a padi, a creek bed in the jungle, or on the slopes of the Nui Dinh Hills.

Ted Harrison had to go down to meet the ship when it came in; he had to see the boys when they arrived on the HMAS *Sydney*. Men who'd shared every aspect of his life—eating, sleeping, patrolling, fighting—were now coming down the gangway of the old aircraft carrier. He was caught up in the huge crowd edging forward. A digger spotted him and grabbed his hand. 'Great to see you, Ted ... gotta see my girlfriend, mate. I'll catch up later.' He was gone.

The veteran stood in the milling mass, watching a thousand hugs and kisses and smiles of relief. He'd risked his life covering their backs, they'd risked theirs covering his. This was the moment they all should have shared. Instead he felt like an alien, like the loneliest man in the world.

Flashback: Ted Harrison—There are 'old man' days—in my twenties! I think about childhood, those golden days when the sun kissed the skin. To go back, just go back and feel it all again; billy cart racing, the 'bitzer' made by Dad from timber scraps and ball bearings; back in Lewisham, where a stick became a sword or a rifle, a dustbin lid became a shield. In rainwater puddles and gutters, leaves and matchboxes became battleships and submarines.

In another place I've been, the rain sluiced down shallow drains that soldiers had dug between the tents at Nui Dat. The sun in that place had not so much burned the skin as sucked at it; sucked out the wetness that crept down the arms and across the face, turned brown from the red dust whipped up by an APC on a narrow road through a quiet village. Look back from the carrier you're on and see the faces of other men, laughing. Look around today; there are no faces I know. But I can still see faces of men with bush hats laughing. If nothing else, I had the pleasure of sharing an experience with the best bunch of men I'll ever meet.

At the Department of Veterans Affairs in St Kilda, Melbourne, Harrison was getting his hearing tested. He had been told by doctors in Vung Tau hospital that his hearing had been damaged in the explosion, and he was now being 'officially' tested. The doctor, in his mid-70s, stood about a metre away and slowly inched forward, whispering, 'What's your middle name?' Crept forward again. 'What's your street number?' The veteran answered correctly. The doctor looked at him, then down at his desk, and scribbled on a pad. 'Nothing wrong with your hearing.'

The second doctor was a cardiologist who sat at his desk negotiating the price of a new car over the phone while his patient removed his shirt. The medico hung up the phone and was about to reach for Harrison's medical file when he noticed the extensive scarring on his patient's body. He walked closer, bent and examined the wounds, then stood up. 'Where did you get the scars, in the real war or in Vietnam, the fake one?'

Harrison was within range for a short jab, or even a powerful uppercut that would have lifted the man's head off his shoulders. Not worth it. Instead he ran down the hall and slammed the door of the toilet cubicle before bursting into tears. *Was this the way it had been with other wars? Old Ted had been in the RAAF during World War II; Grandad was one of the Rats of Tobruk—had they encountered this? Had they felt this emptiness and hollowness inside? It had nothing to do with wounds; it had everything to do with a reaction to an experience—Vietnam. Had they felt this dysfunction and dislocation too ... or was it just me? We pass our use-by date ...*

Ted Harrison sought help many years too late. He came back from the Dark Place where he'd been crouching for years, afraid he was losing his mind. Therapy and medication helped. So did the booze. He took to growing vegetables, and gained enormous pleasure from just watching things grow. There was a problem, though: when the plant was spent, tinged brown and wilting, he couldn't bring himself to pull it out of the soil.

One night at Ted's place, having dinner with an old Army mate, Peter, the conversation gradually turned to Vietnam. Ted's wife, Ursula, listened to the two men for a while, then said, 'Why don't you two talk about something else? Vietnam was a long time ago.'

Peter looked at her for a few seconds without speaking, then quietly replied, 'Ursula, Vietnam will never be a long time ago.'

At 21, Wilf Matusch was granted a half-pension and medical benefits for post-traumatic stress disorder, the loss of central vision in his right eye, and allergic rhinitis (inflammation of the nose membrane). The shrapnel that entered his brain had cut through the orbital and sub-orbital trigerminal nerves, causing partial paralysis on the right side of his face. He shouldn't have survived the wounding; he shouldn't have survived three operations—but he did, with a legacy of a silicon plate under his eye and those 27 silver staples in his skull.

With typical determination, Matusch ignored the seriousness of the brain injury and went back to training men—mainly National Servicemen, and some older than him—who were heading for Vietnam. At the Third Recruit Training Battalion in Singleton, NSW, Matusch found that his nerves had settled: he was able to mix with the other instructors, fellow veterans—good men with a powerful common experience.

Each morning at the instructors' hut, they'd check the roster to see who was doing what with which trainees. One morning, Matusch stood and sipped coffee while the other instructors reminisced about Vietnam. He noticed one was a member of the Armoured Corps, confirmed by the tank badge on his beret. This man was speaking to a small group of comrades. 'I remember the day out on the Firestone Trail we met up with a bunch of Yanks and they'd hit the shit—blown up by mines. We helped them out with a tow and you wouldn't believe it, we only dragged them over another bloody mine. A coupla Yanks were cut up, badly wounded, and I yelled to this bunch of grunts running alongside us to see if there was a medic among them. This bloke puts up his hand, so I tell him to get down and help. You know, that silly bastard actually ran with his medical kit back through the mine-field, patched up the Yanks and carried one onto a chopper. One of the stupidest, gutsiest acts I ever saw. Bloody grunts …'

Matusch smiled to himself.

He was still determined to become an officer. When he enlisted, Matusch had requested Officer Cadet School, and he still wanted to be in the Army—but with a future as an officer and a leader. He sat looking across the desk at the senior officer who was considering his application. 'You see, Corporal Matusch, while you do make an excellent candidate, you were seriously injured in Vietnam.'

You squeezer—as if I can forget that!

'Now we can't be sure, and neither can you, that there won't be any medical problems in the future. If we accept your application and you later have some sort of relapse … we just can't be sure, can we?'

This bloke thinks I might go off my trolley down the track—thinks I'm already a stubbie short of a sixpack. Prick!

The man leaned back and waited for a response, then leaned forward and put his hands together on the desk. He smiled. 'If we retire you at 22, it would mean the Army—the government—would have to pay you a pension for doing nothing for a long time. You'd agree that potentially that's an unfair demand on the public purse, isn't it?'

Matusch struggled for two years to upgrade to full fitness, the standard required for officer training. Then he walked into the office again. This time, the words from the recruiting officer came back to the veteran—York Street, Sydney, August 15, 1967: '… you'll make an excellent officer. Having spent time in the ranks, you'll have real compassion for those in the ranks when you become an officer yourself.'

He looked across the desk again. The words were polite, but firm: 'Corporal Matusch, thank you for the spirit in which you applied. You know, having examined your records, you would make an excellent RSM—next to the CO, the most senior man in a battalion …'

Matusch jumped in. 'Thank you, Sir. My record also shows that I joined the Army at 17 and was to spend two years in the ranks for experience before going to OCS.'

There was a silence, then the officer held up his hand. 'I know. Corporal, you see, you've been in the ranks six years now. You've served in the ranks in a war zone … I'm afraid your psych tests indicate you may have developed an "Other Ranks Tendencies", meaning you may identify too readily with the soldiers you should be leading. I'm sorry, we don't consider you officer material any longer.'

I'VE BEEN AWAY TO WAR

In late September 1971, the 3/33rd North Vietnamese Regiment took a bruising in a series of firefights with elements of 4RAR/NZ(ANZAC). Following a heavy bunker contact with Delta Company, the NVA regulars were withdrawing to the north and north-east of Phuoc Tuy in an attempt to avoid annihilation. Three RAR had been deployed earlier as a blocking force along the eastern edge of the area, while 4th Battalion swept through their AO in an attempt to force the enemy up against the block. Presented with a situation where the enemy had split into three groups and were in apparent disarray, the Australian commanders moved in for the kill: they set down a blocking force ahead of where they believed the enemy was. This was bad news for both the NVA and 3RAR—the latter had only a week remaining of operational duties and a maximum of three weeks left in-country.

This was reason enough for some of the diggers in 3rd Battalion's Charlie Company to feel a bit nervous and angry at the prospect of having to shape up to North Vietnamese troops. The Goons were putting on a typical performance, and the sergeant was tearing out what hair he had left. This time the hair-tearing was shared with a new platoon commander, Lieutenant Peter O'Donnell. 'Pod', as he was called, had only recently joined the battalion, and although the sarge was glad to relinquish the role he'd reluctantly accepted since Dennis Tyson's medivac, he had to be super-vigilant that 'the gang' weren't going to pull a few stunts for the benefit of their new skipper.

The location of the final operation was a piece of worthless, scrubby, isolated high ground overlooking a creek. The Goons were told to dig in. The sergeant had never seen his men work with such zeal—digging was a task they just didn't attack with enthusiasm. More to the point, they were a lot rowdier than usual. Their progress was hampered by the amount of rock in the ground. The small, ineffective entrenching tool—a shovel-pick on a short handle that had not evolved much since World War II—didn't help much, either. The Goons were not really digging the ground, they were killing it. *Whack, whock, crunch, whack, whok, thump, clink, clang …*

As short-timers, they were desperate to get below ground. You only had to listen to their comments to Jacko, who, as usual, was glued to his radio set. 'Sounds like the Nogs are trying to escape, fellas,' Jacko drawled.

'Who gives a stuff if they escape … who gives a fat rat's arse if the whole bloody Noggie army pisses off? The war's friggin' over, mate … and we're going home.'

'Shut up, Woody. Our leaders know what they're doing. You're a soldier, you're here to fight and kill—you're a jungle green-clad killer,' Butch cackled as he bent over and furiously dug around a tree root. The noise he was making was akin to a front-end loader scraping road gravel.

Dixie butted in. 'We've lost the war, givin' it back to the ARVN. Shit, if the ARVN could beat the Nogs, why didn't they do it years ago? We wouldn't have been needed at all. You wait, this country'll go down the gurgler once we leave.'

The platoon commander stopped digging, looked across at the sergeant and asked, 'Hey, Sarge you reckon I ought to do something about the bloody racket the blokes are making?'

The sergeant stopped digging, stood and lit a smoke. 'Noisy little buggers, aren't they, sir? Really, it's almost enough to make a shepherd fuck his flock. You know how to dig a hole in this shit without making a noise?'

The young officer stared back. The sergeant was picking up a head of steam. 'They've got less than three weeks left in this place and they are making noise—you know, I think the idea may be to let the Nogs know we're here. Call it survival—making sure they're not gonna be the last dead diggers in Vietnam. They've got families back home, and as a far as I'm concerned, sir, they're all going back to see 'em again.'

Night came to the small hill. The typical Vietnam night, too still; waiting for something, but what? Not many of the Goons slept that night, and the following morning men reported seeing small moving lights. Fireflies? Others said they heard scrambling on the rocks on the trickling creek just forward and to the side of the hill. *Breathe in, breathe out. Keep silent as a dead man.*

Next morning the platoon moved into the AO. They hadn't travelled more than 100 metres when they came across a fresh track with cuttings on the ground. 'They were here, mate—a bandage ... blood ... by the look of the track they were carrying wounded, too.' Bob Wood was hunched down over the tracks while the Goons nervously eyeballed the surrounding bush. The sergeant also peered into the jungle. *Too right, they were here, and a lot of the bastards at that. The blokes on the M60 did hear things last night. They were probably shitting themselves—if they'd opened up, we'd have certainly been involved in a shit storm. Wonder what stopped the boys from putting on one of their famous 'Yippees' last night ...*

October 1st, 1971, and Charlie Company was given co-ordinates to an LZ for its final lift back to Nui Dat. Never had they moved so quickly, so quietly, so switched on. The slicks appeared like a beautiful dream and the men flung themselves inside, onto the deck, clung to seats and, as if choreographed, each man clutched his rifle like a crutch with his eyes squeezed shut. *Done it! Bloody well done it!*

New greens were issued, bush hats were tucked away—personal items to be carried home—and new boots handed out; the green battalion lanyard was slipped over the shoulder of a shirt that actually smelt new. The battalion citation, a small, blue, rectangular badge with gold edges that was awarded to 3RAR for its legendary stand at the battle of Kapyong in the Korean War, was pinned onto the chest. The Goons drank beer, along with bottles of illicit spirits that had been stashed for RTA celebrations. The platoon logo, a drunken rat clutching a flagon of wine, told the story of the final days. The men smoked, lounged outside the old tents, and grudgingly carried out machine-gun piquet in the sandbagged pillboxes that looked out over the Warburtons. Four days and a wake-up, and morale had slipped—every man had a war hangover.

The sergeant sat in his tent, fidgeting with his final packing. *Two tours, for what? What about all my mates—dead, wounded, fucked in the head, for what? We're no better off today than when I first got off the chopper in '66. We've lost this one. We're deserting the people we got to know in Phouc Tuy and Vungers, and soon it's all gonna go down the shitter. We're pissing off, and these people are going to be done over once the NVA come back—as they surely will.*

Flashback: Goon Sergeant—Remember … remember a girl in a small village out west? She had a baby on her hip. I pledged to protect her when I walked through Xuyen Moc. Remember? I'll pay for my sins. When I get home I'll receive no thanks, be no hero.

Outside the tent, chain-smoking, watching the platoon—my platoon. I'd cut my throat before I come back here. But if I did return, I wouldn't want to be with any other blokes. These men are soldiers, like their fathers, and their fathers before them. They did it hard and did it right. They bitched all the way … just like a good Anzac should …

Jacko made his way to the sergeant's tent, gibbering at 100 miles per hour. When he'd finished, the sergeant softly spoke.

'In case I don't get the chance, Jacko, thanks mate.'

The signaller was taken aback. 'Thanks for what, Sarge?'

The older man reddened. 'Just thanks ... thanks for not asking so many bloody questions, dickhead. Now fuck off.'

The young Nasho turned and pushed out his chest, his Vietnam ribbons and Infantry Combat Badge flashing. 'Hey, Sarge, what do you think? Do I look like a real soldier?'

✳✳✳

The sun came up on a murmuring crowd at the Cenotaph in Sydney's Martin Place, where 3000 Vietnam veterans and their families listened to the Ode of Remembrance read by National RSL President, Sir Colin Hines. It was 7 a.m., Saturday, October 3, 1987. Nearby, in The Domain, there was also a murmur, which by 9 a.m. had become a rolling wall of noise from 35,000 men and women who had to be here, drawn by The Word that had for the past months zipped along the veterans' network—that invisible conduit that carried good and bad news across the nation. *You have to be there ... you are welcome there. You need to be there.* So they came, by car, bus, plane, in wheelchairs, on sticks, in suits, in jeans. Shortly after 9 a.m., the first 520 men and women stepped off to begin their march from The Domain. Each one silently carried an Australian flag—one for each Australian who was killed in action in Vietnam or who died from wounds received. The Vietnam Veterans' Welcome Home Parade had begun.

Colin Cogswell had found his unit, 5RAR, and thought he was ready for the clap and hurrah that was 15 years overdue. What the ex-forward scout and his fellow veterans received was a thunderous roar, a non-stop handclap, a continuous cheer, confetti, streamers and a sea of tears from 110,000 Australians of all ages. They marched down Hunter Street, along Pitt and onto George Street before turning into Bathurst Street. Prime Minister Bob

Hawke took the salute outside the Town Hall, where in June, 1971 the biggest demonstration against the war had been staged.

Cogswell had wandered in a landscape of lost soldiers in the years since his discharge. He fell in love with a woman, Yolanda—that filled some space, but he was still searching. Like many vets, he went bush, taking a job as a plant operator at Copeton Dam in central NSW. Six months later Yolanda came up and they were married in Inverell by the town sheriff. Three years later, Cogswell decided to attend his first Anzac Day, at Inverell. He didn't march, but went to the RSL for a few drinks. To his amazement he met three men he had been working with for the last three years—they were all Vietnam veterans, and no-one had ever mentioned his service. It was, Cogswell recalled, his most memorable Anzac Day, though he later attended others. But, like most Vietnam vets, there was still unfinished business, still the need to *really* come home.

Now that day had come, and it was a day of healing. A little girl waving an Aussie flag, a woman rushing from the crowd to embrace a veteran walking with sticks, a Builders Labourers' Federation banner hung on a skyscraper—'Welcome Home Boys.'

Yes, we were boys.

A soldier stood where the march ended in Hyde Park, and where the veterans dispersed to attend a hundred reunions. In his hand he held a piece of paper with words scribbled by 110 Signal Squadron soldier, Rod Smith.

My country, forgive me,
For I've been away to war.
Remember that you sent me
So please unlock the door.

Colin Cogswell now knew he'd finally come home.

FIRE IN THE SKY

April Fool's Day, 1990, and NSW District Fire Office Alan 'Doggy' Dwyer was certain he was about to die. He had experienced a similar sensation nearly 20 years before, walking through waist-high grass in a clearing in Phuoc Tuy.

Now Dwyer was looking at something he had seen in nightmares, heard about in lectures, and prepared for in training exercises. Four 100-tonne liquid petroleum gas (LPG) tanks were surrounded by fire; the gas relief valve on one was already wide open, shooting a blowtorch of flame 30 metres into the air. The place was the Boral LPG distribution depot in St Peters, Sydney, and the situation was developing so quickly that the firefighters, along with more than a thousand residents within a 2-kilometre radius of the plant, were in grave danger. Passengers on board Ansett flight 601 from Melbourne to Sydney looked down at the blaze and thought a plane had crashed.

On the ground, Dwyer and his team had cut through mesh fences and worked their way to the site with fire trucks. What had appeared as a glow when fire teams got the call was now a vision that would forever burn in their minds.

It started at 20:54 hours on Sunday. A fire crew from Newtown was called to Canal Rd, St Peters. The crew observed smoke, but was unsure of the extent of the blaze on the far side of a warehouse complex. Dwyer had heard 000 calls come through and, with the radio transceiver clutched to his ear, sat in a Fire Brigade sedan while his driver, Kevin 'Moose' Fletcher, pushed the vehicle at full throttle towards the fire. The main pumper truck was also nearing the Boral site; its crew was tearing into the last wire fence with bolt-cutters. The sedan pulled up at the fence and Dwyer struggled to assess the scene before him: the Boral plant had five elevated 100-tonne bulk storage tanks, with hundreds of smaller LPG containers nearby. Unknown to the fire crews, there were another 13 LPG road and rail tankers obscured behind the main fire.

The source of ignition was a manifold system—a mass of steel pipes—beneath the five elevated tanks that was spewing flames upwards. From his vantage point, Dwyer could see that a relief valve on one of the tanks had opened and ignited. The temperature at that point would have been about 1000° Celsius; a flashover to the other tanks and then across the plant would be the equivalent of a small nuclear explosion. In fire veterans' terms, this was the Big One, a conflagration without peer. It was called a BLEVE—a 'Boiling Liquid Expanding Vapour Explosion'—and was a deadly, flaming monster. It levelled blocks of buildings, melted sheet steel, incinerated men and machines. *One flash and we're ash.* You didn't fight and extinguish a BLEVE, you bought time—as much as you could—to get people away. Then you backed off as far as possible before it blew.

Sixteen fire brigades were now at the blaze. As control officer and firefighting strategist, Dwyer had decisions to make that affected the lives of 100 firemen and nearby residents. Sydney Airport and several hotels were also close by, not to mention the usual rubbernecks, already streaming into St Peters to get a look.

No second chance here. Preserve the integrity of those overhead LPG tanks, get them cooled and piss off quick. First, order a civilian evacuation of two to three kilometres. Dwyer got on the radio and started liaising with police and State Emergency HQ. It was 21.15 hours.

The noise from the pressure relief valve sounded to the firefighters—who had brought the water pumper truck to within 45 metres of the fire—as if they were standing behind two 747 jets accelerating for take-off. No-one could speak, no-one could hear. The radiated heat had already melted one radio handset and was almost penetrating Dwyer's outer heavy woollen jacket and burning the skin on his unprotected face. The polycarbonate helmet had no visor.

He moved forward with the lead team. The pumper truck was cranked up, using hydrants inside the complex. A stream of water jetted up and over the five LPG tanks. *I'm not seeing the full picture—there's worse to come,* Dwyer thought. Sure enough, on the western side of the fire, he saw an LPG road tanker—its wheels were on fire.

The main blaze at the manifold intensified, and the venting flame on the large tank shot up another ten metres. The liquid inside the bulk containers was now boiling, and with a *bang! whoosh!* and then a scream, another pressure relief valve ignited. At 21:20, Dwyer's worst fears were realised as the high-pitched scream rose even higher. The situation was now critical: unknown to Dwyer and his team, another 40,000-litre road tanker had ignited on the far side of the main blaze.

The fire chief pulled his handset to his mouth and gave the order for his men to evacuate. 'This is DO 13. Number 13 Pumper, stay in place, unmanned. I repeat order for all members to evacuate. Order also for all civilians to move further back from present evacuation perimeter.'

There was screaming over the handset. 'Get out, gotta get out …'

Some men are losing their nerve. That's understandable. Dwyer snapped the radio up and shouted into it, 'DO 13 here. Listen in. I expect correct radio procedure at all times.' Four men— including his close friend, Senior Station Officer Chris O'Brien—stayed, ensuring everyone evacuated the area.

Dwyer looked through the flames, not at them. *Forward scout: Canungra JTC and Phuoc Tuy. Look through the trees, look beyond, what do you see? Rows and rows of LPG gas storage tanks on railway lines, pointing in all directions. What will happen if they ignite? They'll be propelled like fireballs beyond the LPG farm into civilian areas. Others will become airborne, like rockets leaving a launch pad. Hundreds will be killed. The 100-tonne containers, now overheated to the point of detonation, will compound the disaster.* He yelled again into the radio, instructing the police and the State Emergency Service to move civilians back another kilometre.

If I'm going to die—and it will probably happen any minute—I won't die in panic. I've done my job. I walked across a grass clearing in Vietnam and I was alone. I am out here and alone again … Time to call on all my training. What do I do in a situation like this? I fuck off!

'Chris, Chris! Time for a tactical withdrawal!'

O'Brien turned to see his District Officer waving. The two men ran down the lanes between the warehouses. Panting with exertion and desperate to put space between themselves and the furnace, O'Brien grabbed at Dwyer's coat. 'What did you call this …?'

'A tactical withdrawal.'

'I dunno, Alan, seems to me like we're bloody running.'

By 21:26 Dwyer had reached the muster point one kilometre from the plant. The fires had turned night into day for as far as he could see. Dwyer believed he had bought enough time for the civilian evacuation. He had the pumper going at full kick, punching thousands of gallons of water onto the five overhead cylinders. It was buying time, that's all it was doing; that's all anyone could do. The explosion could come in a heartbeat and it would be spectacular—certainly the biggest bang Sydney had ever seen.

A firefighter called out, 'One man missing. One unaccounted for, Chief.'

Alan Dwyer had put the war behind him. He had gone through the irritations many Vietnam returnees had experienced: the snide remarks, the casual comments about the 'stupid war', and the ignorance of Vietnam and what Aussies were doing there. The ex-scout threw himself into his new job and found it fulfilling. He had also witnessed, in two decades' service with the NSW Fire Brigade, more carnage and horror than he had seen in war: mutilations in car wrecks, suicides, bodies cut in half on railway tracks. He had seen people incinerated. He had also saved some. In addition, he had studied and bettered himself. He had arrived at close to the top of his tree—a District Officer—and had married Jan, a wonderful woman who had given him two daughters. Now every minute of that career, every aspect of fire and its behaviour, had come down to these apocalyptic moments in St Peters.

The Duty Officer had arrived, and was now in earnest discussion with Dwyer over the missing man. Someone had to go back and find him. *Canungra JTC: Make a decision, make a decision and move!* He jerked open the car door while his driver Moose Fletcher opened the other. 'No sense us all getting killed. We'll go,' Dwyer said, and gunned the car back down the lane to the Boral site.

The heat almost melted the windscreen. *Have I used up all my annual leave? How much superannuation have I got racked up? Will Jan and the girls be taken care of?*

Dwyer pushed open the door and turned to Fletcher. 'Ready to find him?'

'I'd follow you into hell, Sir.'

'That's where we're going, Moose.'

The main pumper was still jetting water across the elevated tanks. The fire had now spread from the manifold system and ignited two trucks. The men tried to walk forward and search; there was no use calling out. They both believed they were looking for a body. The inferno facing them had an immediate paralysing effect. The radiated heat forced them to turn and bend at the same time, occasionally dropping to their knees, panting for oxygen. The wheels of the pumper, Dwyer noticed, were beginning to smoke and everything around the men was brilliantly illuminated. Dwyer saw that the stationwagon he had arrived in earlier was parked nearby and seemed undamaged. Still no sign of the missing fireman. *Where the bloody hell is he?* Dwyer made a final assessment of the scene, then the radio inside his jacket crackled. The missing man had found his way back to the muster point.

'In the car—get in the bloody car! He's okay!' Dwyer pulled at Fletcher and the two men dived into separate cars. The vehicles topped 60kmph down the narrow warehouse lanes. Several times Dwyer bounced his car off the walls.

At 21:39 the first of the 40,000-litre road tankers BLEVE'd. The fireball rose hundreds of metres into the night sky and the shockwave almost lifted the fire crews off their feet. At 22:09 there were more explosions, and at 22:17 one of the 100-tonne LPG tanks BLEVE'd. Dwyer could only stare thunderstruck as the tank rose like a bouncing bomb, spiralled 150 metres and slammed down, demolishing an electricity sub-station and a paint and panel shop before crushing the banks of a nearby canal. The concrete footings on which the tank had been anchored were turned to glass by the heat.

Sixteen kilometres away in the suburb of Narwee, Jan Dwyer felt a thump and heard the windows shake. From where she stood, she saw the fireball rise up near Mascot Airport. At Sydney Park, 1000 people who had gathered to watch the fire felt the heatwave roll over them. In many inner-city streets the situation became chaotic as the explosions began while evacuation was still in progress. The BLEVE triggered a domino effect of explosions across the Boral site, detonating hundreds of smaller containers as well as one 45-tonne cylinder. Nine buildings within the 2-hectare site were flattened in the blast or gutted. At Bondi Beach, crowds stood transfixed by the rising fireballs and the orange glow that stretched across the horizon.

As the blasts continued, the Chief Fire Officer arrived on the site to find his District Officer running on empty, drained even of the adrenaline that had kept him on the edge. 'Seems we have more tanks ready to explode and our missing man could be in here,' said the Chief Officer, jabbing at a map he had spread on a car bonnet.

Dwyer pushed the map aside. 'Forget that. Our man's out and there's dozens more tanks than the map shows. And yes, we have a BLEVE.'

The chief stood back and looked at his subordinate. 'Officer Dwyer, these are the plans to the site and we'll use these …'

Dwyer exploded. 'Bullshit, I've looked at what's up there, Sir, and there's many more than shown on that plan.'

The Chief Officer was becoming irritated. 'Well I don't what you've seen and done, but I do know you've left a very expensive pumper truck up there to be destroyed. You do know what they're worth, don't you?'

Dwyer had taken enough.

Flashback: Alan Dwyer—FSB Ziggie, 1971. The officer slides the lid closed over the hot box—'There's no chicken left, digger, you'll have to eat steak.'

Dwyer pushed his face close to the senior officer's. 'Stick your plans up your arse!'

At St Georges Basin, 250 kilometres south of Sydney, there is a collection of small houses and holiday shacks. Most nights, Alan Dwyer sits on the verandah of his home here and looks out across the bay.

It is now more than ten years since the Boral blaze, and 30 years since Vietnam. The irony of the Vietnam experience is not lost on the former soldier: the war had prepared him for the greatest test of his life. He had faced uncertainty and fear in the padis and the jungle, he had learned mateship, loyalty and dedication, and had never really lost his greatest assets—humour and resolve. He had fought with inner demons after the war and suffered post-traumatic stress disorder, but he had soldiered on to become a firefighter—more, a leader of men who faced danger every day. Dwyer and Kevin Fletcher—who collapsed and died suddenly while on duty in 1996—were awarded the country's second highest honour for bravery, the Star of Courage, for their actions during the Boral blaze.

At the age of 46, Dwyer was medically discharged from the Brigade with the rank of Chief Superintendent. Today, the chicken de-beaker who became a forward scout and went on to fight fires has found peace on the coast. He gazes out at dusk over St Georges Basin and watches the sinking sun set fire to the sea.

ENDSTATE

Thirty years after Vietnam, Wilf Matusch's hair had thinned slightly. He carried some extra weight and smoked more than he'd like to. Shorty Mawer was bare-chested, wearing boardshorts, and was looking at the beach while munching toast. He'd been talking about breaks, peaks and the best surfing spots on the east coast. He changed tack between cappuccinos. 'The war buggered my life, you know. I had a paint and panel shop business lined up, a terrific car and a load of girls, and I surfed. I was having a great time. Then came Vietnam and my marble was pulled out.'

I sat with Wilf and Shorty as Wilf started to tell his story. I knew him back in 1967 at the Infantry Training Centre, Ingleburn, where he was a visual tracking instructor. Wilf: solid, strong, at times oh-so naïve, fresh out of school cadets; always the man who stepped forward to help, who put his hand up. He was almost the perfect soldier; exactly what the Army wanted. But he did the one thing you should never do in the Army—he volunteered.

Like I did. My name's Peter Haran. I volunteered to be a dog handler, and took a tracking dog to Vietnam with 2RAR in 1967. On my second tour, with 3RAR, I was a section commander in Anti-Tank Platoon. Alan Doggy Dwyer was my forward scout.

In the early years at the Infantry Centre, Wilf and I used to drive out on Sunday mornings, down to the local Shell cafe to have baked-bean sandwiches. We missed breakfast at the camp so we could eat baked-bean sandwiches. By the time we got back from Vietnam we'd had enough baked beans to start our own natural gas company.

Wilf was also my laundry companion. We hoisted the daggy uniforms down to the laundry in Liverpool for the weekly run, and sat reading 'Phantom' and 'War Picture Library' comics while the clothes washed and dried. I knew Wilf wanted to get ahead in the Army; he enlisted to be an officer, maybe rise to the rank of major. Maybe higher if he went to staff college.

The last time I saw him was in a bed at 2 Military Hospital, over the road from the Infantry Centre. He had been hit in the head by shrap and the doctors here refused to believe a 'MASH' unit surgeon in Vietnam had performed what they called 'a work of art' on his head. They also told Wilf that the non-corrosive silver studs in his skull were worth a fortune, and would be with him for life. We encouraged him to take them out and cash them in, but he didn't plan on it.

Shorty stood, drained his coffee and pushed his chair back. 'I'm going surfing, men. See ya.' He winked and crossed the road to the beach, then Wilf continued.

'You know, Peter, it's taken years to get us all back together again—in our fifties and we're eventually finding each other. What's wrong with us? What went wrong? I tried to forget about Vietnam, but I still get blinding bloody headaches deep behind my right eye that remind me. What's a bit rough, too, is the fact I only ever wanted to be a good soldier …'

'You were a good soldier, Wilf,' I said.

'Yeah, but I wanted to be an officer—to make the service my career. I feel I earned that. But Vietnam blew that plan up as well as blowing me up—twice.' Wilf drank his coffee and lit another cigarette, lost in thought. He looked over to where Shorty was bodysurfing, then continued, 'I really loved the Army; I was infatuated with it. I loved the order, the regimentation, all the history and tradition, pomp and ceremony … those things really meant something to me. I see men I went into the Army with—they've really made it. One's a Brigadier. But I'm happy with my life. I've got two great kids, one's made me a grandfather. And over the past 30 years, Lyn and I have built up an investment business we're proud of.

'But the war was just insane; full of insane things in an insane place. You know, when I got winched out after catching the shrap,

I never saw most of those men again. Some of them thought I only had a few scratches on my face and wanted to get out of the bush, for Heaven's sake. Thirty years later they find out I had brain surgery, 18 hours on the operating table, and in a coma for three days.' He looked at me; almost through me. 'We can't complain too much. Many vets have done well in life. All up, we did our job, Peter—that's what our country wanted of us, and we did it. And a lot men are dead and wounded as a result. But you know, I heard something a while ago that really upset me.'

His eyes moistened as he leant over to me and spoke softly. 'A mate came back from a holiday in Vietnam last year, where he happened to visit one of their war museums. He saw a wartime photo of my mates there—one of those group shots Army PR took. My mate said it wasn't the photo that blew him away, it was the caption underneath in black letters—"AUSTRALIAN WAR CRIMINALS."'

*   *   *

The Blind Welfare Hostel in Adelaide, one morning in 1996, and I was visiting my partner, Liz's, mother. My name's Bob 'Dogs' Kearney. I was the Goon Platoon Sergeant. Before the tour with 3RAR, I served in Vietnam with 5RAR in 1966–67—with Colin Cogswell, Ted Harrison and Trevor Lynch.

I walked into the hostel dining room and immediately noticed a man who was much younger than the other blind people eating at the dining room table—it was Trevor Lynch! I introduced myself.

'Gee, Dogs, it's been a long time. I'm struggling a bit to remember what you looked like … what *do* you look like?'

I tried to describe what I looked like 30 years ago. Handsome? Not really. Rugged? Yeah, maybe, a bit rough round the edges. We walked back to Trevor's room, with him gently feeling his way along the wall. He opened the door and pushed a chair towards me. 'Here Dogs, sit down for a while.'

He offered me a cigarette. 'I tried to give 'em up. Did for a while, but there's not much to do so I took 'em up again.' He smiled. I looked into his eyes: they weren't eyes, they were porcelain cosmetic replacements that didn't sit quite right. One looked left, the other swivelled right.

'Do you follow the horses at all, Dogs?' He felt along the table for the ashtray.

'No, mate, one thing I never got interested in.'

'Just going to listen to this race, mate. Take it easy for a minute.' Trevor felt around for his small transistor radio and flicked it on. He was trying to light another cigarette and I watched as he felt for the end before lighting it. Even then he lit it part-way along.

I looked around his small unit. Off the bedroom was a shower and toilet. The only furniture in the main room was a table, two chairs, a bed, a set of drawers and a built-in wardrobe. Nothing else. What else would a man with no eyes want? Trev had no need for pictures, TV, a magazine rack …

He listened to the race. I began to feel overwhelmed with sadness—this man had lived in total blackness since that day in the Nui Thi Vai mountains in October, 1966, 30 years ago. He'd been in here since his loving mum died.

'Anything you need, Trev?'

'Not really, mate. Sometimes my ex-Army mates drop in and, if I do need anything special, they get it for me. My family comes and sees me when they're in town. So, you see, I've got pretty much all I need.'

All he needs. Most people in here are in their seventies—he has to endure sitting at a table twice a day with blind people who for most of their lives were fully sighted, until old age got to them. I looked down and noticed the state of his trousers. Between the knees and waistband were dozens of tiny holes where hot cigarette ash had dropped and burned through the trouser cloth, unnoticed until he felt his skin burning.

I went back to see Trevor as often as I could, and most times found him hunched over his small table puffing furiously on a cigarette as he listened to the races. *All he's got in the world—a bloody radio.* I desperately wanted to give him something to make his life more bearable. He didn't need money or anything material, he needed a life. One day, out of my need to do something, I asked, 'What's the tucker like in here, Trevor?'

'Not too bad, Dogs. They change the menu around a fair bit.'

'Which meals do you like best?'

'I used to love Mum's cooking. But since she went, I eat pretty well anything on the table. My favourite dish would be banana fritters. I haven't had those in a very long time … like 'em with fish and chips and lots of salt wrapped in paper. We don't get them here. I suppose it's not something the oldies go for …'

I nodded at Liz and she nodded back and asked, 'Want to come to our place for fish and chips and banana fritters, Trev?' Tears were welling in her eyes.

'You mean the bought ones from the fish shop, Liz?'

Back home, Trevor sat at the kitchen table and scoffed down enough fish and chips to feed a small orphanage. He saved the fritters until last.

We kept visiting Trevor, and asked him home again, but he never came. He felt safe at the hostel, among other blind people. I contacted a few veteran mates, and one of them—Ken 'Kojak' Chester, ex-Australian Army Training Team—started to visit Trevor regularly. Trev started to go to veterans' barbecues, and his old 5RAR mates as well as some other friends took him out for Anzac Day, where he took pride of place at the front of the battalion in his wheelchair.

The biggest thrill of all for Trevor was when the Vietnam Veterans' Motorcycle Club came to the hostel and took him for a ride in a sidecar. Trevor was rapt when they came again. He whispered to Chester, 'Get the blokes to rev the bikes up when they leave, will you? I want the people in here to know the sort of mates I've got.'

One day at a barbecue with the bike club I noticed that Trevor's skin colour had changed to a sort of yellow. 'What gives?' I asked Kenny Chester.

'He's dying, mate. Cancer of the liver. He wants to keep it quiet for a while until he gets used to the idea himself.'

'Dyin' of cancer, you can't be bloody serious! For God's sake, child molestors live till they're a bloody hundred and a digger who never hurt anyone in the entire world cops this lot. Not fair, Ken, just not bloody fair.' I was so upset, I felt ill.

I went to the Repatriation Hospital at Daw Park on a number of occasions and took Colin Cogswell with me. I had a Harley. Trevor whispered, 'Rev the Harley. I know it's only for a few seconds, Dogs, but I like to tell them in here that my mates are bikies.'

I revved it again when I left and on every other visit.

On my last visit, with Cogswell, it was apparent that Trev wanted to talk more than he normally did. 'I get a bit lost, you know, Dogs. Lucky I had some great mates around after Mum died. She was a lovely lady and a fantastic mum. We had a lot of good years together before she died. When she went, the only place for me was the Blind Welfare. My family's been very supportive, but they've all got jobs and kids and live way out in the country—and I needed to be close to the Repat Hospital. Trouble is, I have difficulty dealing with strange places … Will you take me to the toilet? I need a piss.'

Colin stood and said, 'I know where it is, Trev …'

I jumped in, 'S'okay Cogsy, you make a coupla brews and I'll take him.'

I let Trevor take me by the elbow as I led the way. He was wearing one of the hospital gowns that tie at the back, and when we reached the toilet he asked, 'Would you mind pointing my dick at the bowl, please Dogs?'

I aimed Trevor at the bowl, and for the first time saw up close what the booby-trap shrapnel had done to him. His body was a mass of scar tissue and his forehead was pitted with holes, as if someone had fired a shotgun into his face at close range.

I led him back to bed and he lay there, not touching his coffee. After a few minutes he said, 'Dogs, will you hold my hand, please?' I pulled a chair up to the bed and took his hand.

'Dogs, they reckon I've got brain damage. You don't reckon I've got brain damage, do you?'

'No mate, bullshit. The squeezers got you mixed up with some other bloke. You're as bright as a button.'

There was more silence, then he turned towards me. 'Dogs, I don't have too many regrets, but there is one.'

'What's that, Trev?'

'I'd like to have had the chance to get married and have a family of my own. Do you think I'll get another go?'

Tears were streaming down my face. I could only squeeze his hand and croak, 'Shit, mate, you're special. Next time you'll be rich, have lots of kids and, who knows, maybe you'll even be a movie star.'

Trevor slipped back onto his pillow. 'I hope you're right, Dogs. I really didn't get much of a go, did I, mate?'

THE END

EPILOGUE

Colin Cogswell MM now lives in Adelaide. He is Totally and Permanently Incapacitated (TPI). He said during the writing of this book: 'Vietnam changed our lives, certainly, but I feel honoured to stand in the company of all Vietnam veterans—most of whom, despite a great deal of adversity, have gone on to become model citizens and outstanding Australians.'

Alan 'Doggy' Dwyer SC retired from the NSW Fire Brigade, where he was awarded the Star of Courage for bravery during the 1990 Boral LPG fire. He now lives at St Georges Basin with his wife, Jan. He is also TPI.

Alex Goulevitch MID. The radio operator was Mentioned in Dispatches for his courage during the booby-trap incident and dustoff action on August 8th, 1970 in Long Kahn province. These days he is actively involved in veterans' welfare through the Brisbane chapter of the Vietnam Veterans Motorcycle Club, whose support has helped him over the years.

Jimmy Griffiths discovered a lump on his back just days before he attended the thirtieth reunion of 3RAR's departure for South Vietnam, in April 2001. The old padmaster who devoted his time to the orphans of Dat Do died of cancer on 1 June 2002. He is survived by his wife, Helga, their children and grandchildren.

Edmund 'Ted' Harrison is TPI and lives in Melbourne with his wife, Ursula. He has a son and a daughter. He has spent the past few years building a website about 5th Battalion, the unit he served with. Ted also is a regular blood donor, 'giving something back to the people who gave me five units of blood in Vietnam and saved my life.'

Roly Horopappera MM. The New Zealander section commander, Corporal in Victor Company, RNZIR—one of two New Zealand companies attached to 2RAR/NZ(ANZAC) during the 1970–71 tour of duty—was awarded the Military Medal for bravery during an attack on an enemy bunker system in July, 1970 in Phuoc Tuy. On his return to New Zealand, he remained in the Army, reaching the rank of Sergeant and becoming Instructor of Recruits at the RNZIR Training Depot, Waiouru. Roly died of cancer in the late 1980s.

Trevor Lynch died on 8 April 1997. At the funeral they played his favourite Jimmy Little song, 'Telephone To Glory'. Trevor would have been happy to see quite a few veterans on motorbikes present on the day he was laid to rest.

Wilf Matusch His aspirations of a military career over so soon after enlisting, Wilf requested his discharge from the Australian Army early into his second term of re-engagement, to pursue a business career in the financial services sector. Together with his wife Lyn and their son and daughter they settled in Tweed Heads early in 1982, where they watched their two children grow into successful young adults. At the time of writing this book Wilf still works in the successful, growing Corporate Financial Planning Practice he and Lyn founded many years ago. They continue to enjoy close contact with their children and their children's families.

Bob 'Woody' Wood lives in Canberra and works with the Department of Housing. He has established a website featuring Charlie Company, 3RAR, which is a favourite of many veterans—particularly those of the Goon Platoon.

GLOSSARY

GENERAL

1,2,3, etc, RAR: Battalions of the Royal Australian Regiment (Infantry).

25-set: AN/PRC 25 VHF man-portable radio set.

1ATF: First Australian Task Force, based at Nui Dat.

A-4: Army charge sheet brought against a soldier for military offence.

AFVN Radio: American Armed Forces Radio station Saigon.

Beaucoup: French-Vietnamese word used to describe a 'lot' or 'many.'

Betel juice: Red juice secreted from betel nut when chewed (mild narcotic).

C-4 plastic: Explosive, usually triggered by detonator and fuse, used to destroy enemy bunkers.

Casevac: Casualty evacuation by dustoff helicopter.

Charlie: The Vietcong, also known as Victor Charlie, or VC.

Click: 1000 metres.

CO: Commanding Officer.

Digger: Australian soldier.

Dustoff: Evacuation of the wounded or sick by helicopter.

FAC: Forward Air Controller, flew light aircraft to call in air strikes.

FO: Forward artillery observer who travels with infantry to direct artillery fire.

FSB: Fire support base established as an artillery position in the field during operations.

Grunt: Affectionate term to describe infantry soldier.

Harbour: Defensive position adopted by section or platoon of infantry usually during night stop on operations.

KIA: Killed in action.

Locstat: Location Statement, map reference indicating where a company or platoon is in the field.

Looey: Lieutenant.

Napalm: Highly inflammable incendiary bomb.

Medivac: Medical evacuation from the field through illness.

Nasho: National Serviceman.

NCO: Non-Commissioned Officer.

Nog: Derogatory term used by Australians to describe the enemy. American equivalent: gook.

NVA: North Vietnamese Army regular troops.

OC: Officer commanding a major unit.

Piquet: Sentry duty.

Platoon (Australia): One officer and 33 other ranks.

Platoon (Vietnam): Two thirds of the above.

Punji pit: Pit containing sharpened stakes.

RAP: Regimental Aid Post.

Recce: Reconnaissance to survey or probe enemy presence.

Resup: Resupply in the field of rations and water.

RSL: Returned Serviceman's League.

RTA: Return To Australia.

Rules of Engagement: Procedure for firing on suspected enemy.

Sapper: A soldier from the Royal Australian Engineers (RAE).

SAS: Special Air Service.

Section: 10 infantry soldiers. Usually 6 or 8 in Vietnam.

Shellscrape: Small scrape dug by soldiers to get below ground level.

Shrapnel: Flying fragments from bomb or artillery shell.

Sig: Signaler or radio operator, carries the 25-set.

Sitrep: Situation report by radio from soldiers in the field.

Slick: Troop-carrying helicopter.

Stokes Litter: Special stretcher used to winch casualty from the field.

TAOR: Tactical Area of Responsibility.

Tracer: A round that provides a red or green glow at the rear to enable soldiers to see the round's trajectory.

VC: Viet Cong, described phonetically as Victor Charlie in radio transmission.

Web belt: A belt from which a soldier hangs water bottles and ammunition pouches.

WIA: Wounded in action.

WO: Warrant officer.

Weed: Slang term for out in the field, usually the jungle. Also the scrub.

WEAPONS—GUNS

Artillery: Howitzer, from 105mm to 175mm.

Armalite: Lightweight, American-made 5.56mm automatic rifle.

AK-47: Fully automatic 7.62mm enemy assault rifle.

Bandolier: Shoulder-carried ammunition pouch.

Bofor: Rapid firing 40mm gun.

Canister round: Anti-personnel round fired by tanks or artillery.

Claymore mine: Command-detonated explosive device loaded with small steel balls. Bank of claymores: Three or more set to detonate with det cord.

Det cord: Instantaneous explosive fuse.

Fifty Cal: .50 calibre heavy machine gun.

Flamethrower: Weapon carried by Assault Pioneers firing flame to clear caves or bunkers.

Gatling gun: Six-barreled 7.62mm machine gun with fire rate of 6500 rounds per minute.

GPMG: General purpose 7.62mm belt-fed machine gun carried by infantry section.

Howitzer: See artillery.

Jumping Jack: M16 antipersonnel mine.

Mini-gun: See gatling.

M-26: High explosive fragmentation grenade.

M-60: See GPMG.

M-79: Shotgun-style weapon fired 40mm bombs.

M-72: Light-weight, shoulder-supported, 66mm high explosive anti-tank rocket launcher.

RPG: Shoulder-launched rocket propelled grenade used by enemy. Also RPG2, RPG7

SLR: Self Loading Rifle, semi-automatic standard Australian infantry weapon.

Smoke grenade: Non-explosive grenade which emits various colours of smoke to mark LZ or contact zone.

AIRCRAFT AND TRANSPORT AND ARMOUR

APC: Armoured Personnel Carrier used as troop carrier or assault vehicle.

B52: Heavy US strategic bomber carrying 500–1000lb bombs.

Bird Dog: Cessna reconnaissance aircraft.

Bushranger: Australian helicopter gunship, usually modified Iroquois.

C-130: Long range heavy transport aircraft with four engines. Known as Hercules.

C-123: Smaller version of C-130 Hercules (Called Baby Herc).

Canberra Bombers: Australian jet bombers also used for air photography.

Caribou: Twin-engined light transport aircraft (also known as Wallaby).

Centurian: Australia's main battle tank during the Vietnam War (also known as 'Cent').

Cheyenne: Medium-sized high-speed observation helicopter.

Chinook: Large twin-rotored transport helicopter (CH-47).

Coyote: Small high-speed recce helicopter made by Hughes Corporation.

Chopper: General term for all helicopters.

Gunslinger: American helicopter gunship. See Bushranger.

Hercules: See C-130.

Huey: Iroquois helicopter, Bell model UH-1H, used as multi-purpose aircraft in Vietnam.

Iroquois: See Huey.

Kiowa: Light observation helicopter similar to jet Ranger made by Bell.

Lamboretta: Three-wheeled motorbike used as a taxi.

Sioux: Light utility aircraft used for observation and command.

Sky Crane: Large helicopter made by Sikorsky, used to lift and carry heavy loads.

Starlifter: Largest aircraft in Vietnam, used as long-range jet transporter.

MILITARY TERMS AND ACRONYMS

ANZAC: Australian New Zealand Army Corps.

AATV: Australian Army training Team Vietnam.

1ALSG: 1st Australian Logistic Support Group, based at Vung Tau.

1AFH: Ist Australian Field Hospital, based at Vung Tau.

2IC: Second in command.

ARVN: Army of the Republic of Vietnam.

AO: Area of operations.

Cheap Charlie: Vietnamese term for Digger who refuses to buy drinks.

CHICOM: Chinese Communist.

MM: Military Medal, award for bravery.

OPDEM: Operational Demand for equipment.

O Group: Orders Group to convey commander's intent.

PF: Provincial Force, South Vietnamese Army.

PTSD: Post Traumatic Stress Disorder, trauma condition following combat service.

RV: Rendezvous or meeting up place.

RMO: Regimental Medical Officer (doctor).

AUTHORS' NOTES

For further information on *Flashback*, *Crossfire* and *Trackers* go to the author's website: www.vietnam-crossfire.com or email: kearneyr@chariot.net.au. This site will also connect you to the official 5RAR website by Brian London OAM DCM, the Ted Harrison website and The Goon Platoon website.

ABOUT THE AUTHORS

PETER HARAN joined the Army in 1966 and first served in Vietnam during 1967–68 with 2nd Battalion Royal Australian Regiment, attached to a combat tracking team. As one of the first Australian dog handlers, he wrote of his experiences with tracking dog Caesar in the highly successful book *Trackers: The Untold Story of the Australian Dogs of War* (New Holland, 2000) and later co-wrote *Crossfire: An Australian Reconnaissance Unit in Vietnam* with colleague Robert Kearney. After two years as a dog trainer with the Army's Tracking Unit in Sydney, Peter served a second tour in Vietnam as an infantry section commander with 3rd Battalion in 1971. He left the Army in 1972, and is now a journalist with the Adelaide *Sunday Mail*.

ROBERT KEARNEY joined the Army in 1963 and was a member of Airborne Platoon with 1st Battalion before his first tour of Vietnam with 5th Battalion, where he was a section commander with Reconnaissance Platoon. His second tour of duty was with 3rd Battalion as rifle company platoon sergeant. Bob went on to serve as an instructor at the Army's Jungle Training Centre, 2 Commando Company, and was later a training officer at Officer Cadet School, Portsea Victoria. After his full-time military service, Bob joined the Correctional Services Department and later became a prison manager. He was awarded the Correctional Services Exemplary Conduct Medal for courage and leadership as a hostage negotiator during a 1996 prison riot. Today he is a training consultant, working with the South Australian Country Fire Service and the State Emergency Service volunteers. He is also an Infantry Rifle Company Commander with the Army Reserve 10/27th Battalion, based in Adelaide. Bob co-authored *Crossfire* with Peter Haran.

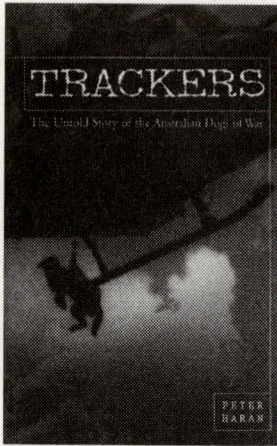

Trackers: The untold story of the Australian dogs of war is the gritty and moving account that reveals the Australian Army's little-known use of combat tracker dogs during the Vietnam War. Author, Peter Haran, recounts his 'tour' of Vietnam with vivid and compelling immediacy, blending the terror of hunting the elusive Viet Cong with the tender relationship between him and his larrikin labrador-kelpie-cross, Caesar.

A graphic portrayal of the timeless reality of war—the horror, the madness, the tedium, the dark humour—*Trackers* hurls you into a surreal world of seething jungles, random minefields, and lethal 'friendly fire'. Amid the mayhem, Peter finds vital refuge in Caesar's playful innocence.

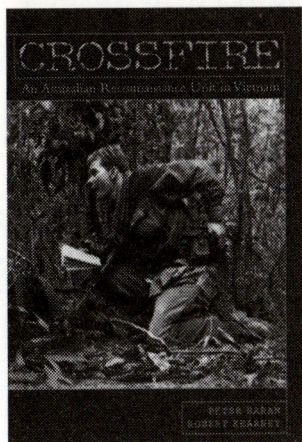

In October 1966, a group of 28 soldiers was chosen to form Australia's first specialist Reconnaissance Platoon in the Vietnam War. One of this platoon's section commanders was a 20-year-old regular soldier named Bob Kearney, who led a series of deadly patrols while the First Australia Task Force established its headquarters in South Vietnam. Operating in isolation and extreme danger ahead of the main Australian forces, these young men braved regular enemy contacts, mines, booby traps, and the natural perils of the teeming jungle. *Crossfire: An Australian reconnaissance unit in Vietnam* is the story of Bob and his unit—a tale of courage, terror, madness amd survival.

Like mosty veterans, the war didn't end for Bob and his fellow soldiers when their tour of duty was done: it haunted them night and day for decades. The lifelong bond forged between these men in Vietnam sees them unite 30 years later in the silent vastness of the Australian Outback. Reliving the fears, the desperation and the camaraderie of war, they finally lay their crippling ghosts to rest.

What the critics said about *Crossfire* and *Trackers*:

'*Trackers grabs you from the very first page and leaves you almost in tears by the end … the writing captures the full range of emotions, trials and situations faced by Australian infantry soldiers in Vietnam brilliantly and is another fine example of the Aussie approach to war-fare—sheer professionalism lavished with large doses of humour.*'
Jason Logue, *ARMY* Magazine

'*… superbly written memoirs of military isolation …* Crossfire *is as unstable and disorienting as the life soldiers led in Vietnam.*'
Michael Thomas, *Wartime*, Australian War Memorial

'Crossfire *not only holds the interest all the way, but in many places reads like a best-selling novel.*'
Amazon.com

'*Trackers is by no means a comforting and gentle musing about man's best friend. It is a compelling and frequently horrifying account of the Vietnam War through the eyes of the author, Peter Haran. A wonderful and frightening book which honours his own powerful memories, his fellow soldiers … and a dog with attitude called Caesar.*'
Frances Atkinson, the *Age*